MW00675362

INTERNATIONAL SHOPPING CENTER ARCHITECTURE

INTERNATIONAL SHOPPING CENTER ARCHITECTURE

Details, Concepts & Projects

Ronald A. Altoon, FAIA

RETAIL REPORTING CORP., NEW YORK

Copyright © 1996 by International Council of Shopping Centers

All rights reserved. No part of this book may be reproduced in any form or by any electronic or mechanical means, including information storage and retrieval systems, without permission in writing from the publisher.

Retail Reporting Corporation
302 Fifth Avenue
New York, NY 10001

Distributors to the trade in the United States and Canada
McGraw-Hill, Inc
1221 Avenue of the Americas
New York, NY 10020

Distributors outside the United States and Canada
Hearst Books International
1350 Avenue of the Americas
New York, NY 10019

Library of Congress Cataloging in Publication Data:
International Shopping Center Architecture, Details, Concepts & Projects

Printed in Hong Kong
ISBN 0-934590-81-8

Book Design: Harish Patel Design
Cover Design Mary Tiegreen

CONTENTS

FOREWORD

In a corridor at an ICSC meeting in Mexico City in 1993, Ron Altoon and I started talking about the central theme of this book. Certain principles of shopping center design and architecture as well as certain basics of center operation translate easily from place to place, country to country, culture to culture. This can happen in some instances with little or no adaptation. Other things don't move as easily or at all, unless they are modified and fitted carefully to the local scene.

The place where retailing occurs needs to be attractive, welcoming. It does not always have to be familiar, indeed at times the newness of the place, the difference in how the offer is made, may be a major element of the attraction. The package, the environment, is what the architect and designer strive to address. That is what this book is principally about. Its many photos show some of the most striking examples of positive adaptation in details of items that are themselves more or less universal where shopping centers, particularly malls, are concerned.

What this book shows, and what a presentation Ron Altoon and I did together at the Second ICSC World Congress of Shopping Centers in Vienna in the spring of 1995 and again at the Third ICSC Asia Conference in Singapore in late October 1995 attempted to make clear, is that there are remarkable parallels between the sort of physical elements of the retail package—the center—that are the focus of this book and how that package is managed and maintained.

When a package is simply copied, as if it were picked up in one place and set down intact in a different place, the center has tended to have a hard time—indeed even to fail. Where the building is confused with its purpose, merchandising, or when the wrong merchandising is forced into a package ill-suited to promote it, the result can be an unhappy one. Nowhere in the world, despite valiant and on-going attempts to prove otherwise, has the condominium approach to center ownership worked. However, everywhere in the world where management control is clear-cut and management itself up-to-date and on task, there centers flourish almost without regard to the nature of the ownership of the property.

All of that is perhaps the stuff of still another book to see the light in another day. In the meantime, here for the eye and the brain are both a beautiful book and a thoughtful presentation, a close look at the package and in particular its details. You'll want to turn the pages slowly.

John T. Riordan
President
International Council of
Shopping Centers

PREFACE

I've been designing and trying to understand shopping centers since 1973. In my years as partner for design in one of the largest American architectural firms specializing in retail buildings, I've had the opportunity to work with America's most prominent developers. Working in every part of the country, I was fortunate to lead the design effort on some of America's most prominent retail projects. From the mid-eighties to the mid-nineties, few new retail centers were being developed. My work therefore became that of renovating, expanding, and repositioning existing buildings.

From that perspective, I had the opportunity to learn firsthand which aspects of buildings, that is, which design decisions, endure time, and which must be reconsidered due to the lack of endurance. I broke down the regional shopping center into small parts and examined the durability of each element and detail.

Along with these evaluations was a desire among many of my clients to create prototypes that did not formerly exist in the retail vocabulary. Many of the lessons for these were emerging in Europe and parts of Asia. Through a stroke of fortune, my professional career has kept me traveling from continent to continent fairly consistently since the late 1970s. This has afforded me an opportunity to compare the American experience with that in other places.

The idea of translating ideas across borders became an imperative for all of us involved in the international business environment, but with differences in the availability of land and costs, construction techniques, and business formats, all inflicting a common prototype, it was clear that it was not the prototype that could translate, but the elements that comprised it. This book is intended to facilitate the translation of ideas from country to country, culture to culture, and place to place.

Ronald A. Altoon, FAIA
Partner
Altoon + Porter Architects
Los Angeles, California
January 1996

ACKNOWLEDGMENTS

The author wishes to acknowledge all the members of the retail industry who have provided the opportunity to learn about this extraordinary public building type, who have willingly shared their knowledge and information with me for more than twenty years. Developers, leasing agents, management, security and operations personnel, architects, consulting engineers, lighting designers, landscape architects, graphic designers, lawyers, department store representatives, and merchants have all contributed to a knowledge base that is constantly in flux and always stimulating. All these professionals are brought together with remarkable frequency due to the organizational skills at the International Council of Shopping Centers (ICSC). John T. Riordan, President of ICSC, has guided the organization through much of the time of my active involvement, and it is to him I am most indebted for affording me the opportunity to attend the 2nd ICSC World Congress of Shopping Centers in Vienna, in 1995, to share the podium with him, and to jointly deliver our combined effort, accompanied by hundreds of slide images. Lastly, to my partners and associates at Altoon + Porter Architects with whom I collaborate daily and share a common passion, to these architects with whom I compete and who keep me focused and inventive, I am much obliged.

PHOTO CREDITS

Grateful acknowledgment is made to the following individuals and companies for permission to reproduce photographs and plans:

Al Ghurair Shopping Centres, Bur Juman Centre, Al Harthy Complex: Pages 102 A, 186–187, 188–189, 190.

Rick Alexander and Associates Inc.: Pages 94 A, 136–137. © Rick Alexander.

Ronald A. Altoon, FAIA: Pages 17 A–F, 18–19 A–D, 20 A, 27 F, 28B, 29 B, 42–43 A–B, 45 B, 46 B, 48 A, 58 A, 65 A, 67 C–D, 68 B, 69 C, 71 C, 72 A, 73 B, 77 B, 79 E, 80 A, 82 B, 83 C, 84 A, 85 B, 88 A, 90 B, 91 A, D–F, 97 B, 191 A, E–F. © 1995 Ronald A. Altoon.

Altoon + Porter Architects: Pages 23 A–B, 24–25 A–D, 26 A–B, 92–93 A–D.

Anthony Belluschi Architects, Ltd.: Pages 37 C, 41 B, 78 B, 184–185.

The Bentall Center: Pages 166–167.

Paul Bielenberg Photography/RTKL Associates, Inc.: Pages 39 B, 75 B, 80 B, 99 C, 101 B, 138–139, 142–143, 184–185. © Paul Bielenberg.

CitraLand Mall: Pages 174–175.

CK Architectural Photography: Page 31C. © Cathy Kelly.

Ann Davidson: Pages 27B, 85 C, 91 B, 100A, 104 A. © Altoon + Porter Architects.

Development Design Group: Pages 176–177.

ELS/Elbasani & Logan Architects: Pages 170–171.

David FranzenPhotography: Pages 28 A, 55 E, 56 A, 81 C, 88 C, 118–119, 191 C. © 1995 David Franzen.

Taizo Furukawa: Pages 172–173.

Brian Gassel/Thompson, Ventulett, Stainback & Associates, Inc.: Pages 27 D, 32 A, 35 C, 38 A, 47 C, 53 B, 54 B, 68 A, 79C, 87 B, 88 B, 89 E, 126–127, 128–129.

Tim Griffith/RTKL Associates, Inc.: Pages 30 B, 55 C, 182–183.

Heuvel Galerie: Pages 168–169.

Robert G. Holt/Arrowstreet Inc.: Pages 34 A, 36 A, 44 A, 52 A, 57 D, 66 B, 78 A, 82 A, 83 D, 122–123, 144–145, 152–153, 154–155. © 1995 Robert G. Holt.

R. Greg Hursley, Inc.: Pages 33 B, 99 B. © Greg Hursley.

Timothy Hursley: Pages 29B, 30 A, 51 C, 54 B, 55 D, 79 D, 96 A, 120–121, 124–125. © Timothy Hursley.

The Jerde Partnership: Pages 27 B, 95 B, 140–141.

Jane Lidz Photography: Pages 39 C, 46 A, 49 B, 50 B, 57 C, 58 B, 66 A, 76 A, 91 C, 112–113, 191 D. © Jane Lidz.

Mark Lohman Photography: Page 105 B. © Mark Lohman.

Juan Carlos Lopez & Asociados S.A.: Pages 109F, 158–159, 160–161, 162–163.

Maxwell MacKenzie/RTKL Associates, Inc.: Pages 101 C, 130 Top, 131.

Mall of America: Pages 64 B, 102 B, 103 C–D.

Greg Matulionis Photography: Pages, 36 B, 54 A, 59 C, 71 B, 75 C, 90 A. © Greg Matulionis.

Charles Mayer: Pages 62 A, 91 F. © Charles Mayer Photography.

Alise O'Brien: Pages 35 D, 85 D, 132–133, 156–157.

Ringstrassen Galerien: Pages 164–165.

RTKL Associates, Inc.: Pages 63 B, 178–179.

Sclater Kimball Architects: Pages 109 B, 110–111, 114–115.

William Sebring: Page 60 A. © Altoon + Porter Architects.

Spillis Candela & Partners, Inc.: Page 61 B.

Wayne Thom Photographer: Pages 27 C, 34 B. © Wayne Thom.

Wes Thompson/RTKL Associates, Inc.: Pages 74 A, 109 E, 180–181, 191 B.

Peter Vanderwalker: Page 40 A.

D. Whitcomb/RTKL Associates, Inc.: Pages 86 A, 89 F, 106 A, 130 Bottom, 146–147, 148–149.

Zeidler Roberts Partnership/Architects: Pages 27 A and E, 45 C, 50 A, 56 B, 70 A, 89 D, 109 A, C–D, 116–117, 134–135, 150–151.

ABOUT THE AUTHOR

Ronald A. Altoon is a founding partner of Altoon + Porter Architects. As Partner-for-Design he has primary responsibility for establishing design concepts and directing evolving design schemes in master planning, urban design, and architecture on all projects worldwide. A native of Los Angeles, Mr. Altoon received his Master of Architecture degree from the University of Pennsylvania and his Bachelor of Architecture degree from the University of Southern California.

Since the formation of Altoon + Porter Architects in 1984, Mr. Altoon has led the design efforts on many award-winning retail and mixed-use projects for many world-renowned clients/developers. Five of these projects have won ICSC awards for design excellence in the past six years.

Mr. Altoon has been actively involved in professional, educational, cultural, and civic enterprises throughout the United States and since 1977 has practiced in the international arena of Asia, Southeast Asia, South America, Mexico, the Middle East, and the former Soviet Union.

Currently a vice president of the American Institute of Architects, he organized and led AIA's disaster assistance design efforts to aid the Soviet Union after the devastating 1988 earthquake. For these efforts he was awarded the Memorial Medal by the Supreme Soviet of the Republic of Armenia.

INTERNATIONAL SHOPPING CENTER ARCHITECTURE

UNDERSTANDING THE INTERNATIONAL SHOPPING CENTER ENVIRONMENT

All around the globe, shopping centers exhibit both similarities and differences from country to country. But any desire to implant a highly refined foreign prototype into another venue soon leads to the realization that some center designs and retail concepts travel well, while others must be adapted to local conditions. In each country special local knowledge and skills are required when retail is combined with office, residential, entertainment and recreational facilities.

One common approach is to view shopping centers first as buildings, and only subsequently as unique locations and places in which retailing occurs. With respect to both center design and retail approach, concepts that are or appear to be successful in one part of the world may not succeed in another. The failure to adapt appropriately to local conditions can produce very poor results.

A

B

C

D

E

F

A. *Floating Market Bangkok, Thailand*

B. *Jitney Bus Philippines*

C. *Pottery Studio Guadalajara, Mexico*

D. *Umbrella Bangkok, Thailand*

E. *Vegetable Market Seattle, Washington*

F. *Fruit Market Hong Kong*

Like the details of buildings, the cultural elements that shape people's lives create the context within which shopping center projects succeed or fail. These cultural elements demand sensitivity and attention. In searching for a place to begin, one should not overlook the traditional marketplaces that are a part of many cultures. Such institutions as the bazaar, the suk, the mercado and the swap meet flourish with intensity and provide an energy level that those involved with shopping centers should seek to learn from them.

A

B

A. *Basket Market Guadalajara, Mexico*

B. *Pot and Pan Market Hong Kong*

C. *Vegetable Market Seattle, Washington (Opposite)*

D. *Floating Market Bangkok, Thailand (Opposite)*

Experience has shown that many general retail concepts translate across borders, across oceans, and across cultures. But, it is also clear that specific solutions often do not. National laws governing imports and exports, licensing, and copyright and trademark infringement prevent the specific replication of retail merchandise and merchandising concepts from country to country and culture to culture. This is a critical factor, as strong anchor merchants, which energize and give functional form to shopping centers in one country, may be precluded from participating in shaping centers in another.

C

D

In considering what travels well and what doesn't, a common international "language" for center retailing is invaluable, that is, a method by which successful ideas can be spoken about in virtually all lands. This book, with the aid of many images, in effect proposes an international language of retail buildings. The grammar of this language is simple; the vocabulary is concise. The language crosses every business and cultural situation and creates a common standard upon which the shopping center industry can rely and flourish.

A. *Oriental Door Handle Japan*

A

THE WORLD ECONOMY AND DEMOGRAPHICS

For the purposes of shopping center development, it is most useful to divide the globe roughly along the equator, that is, along a north/south axis rather than the usual east/west axis. In the broadest terms, the northern hemisphere (North) is richer than the southern hemisphere (South), and its population is older with slower growth.

On a per capita basis, income in the North is dramatically higher and more evenly distributed than in the South. To be sure, there are rich and poor in both hemispheres, but the distance between the two is closer in the North than in the South.

These facts are well known. Yet in country after country in the South, the first wave of modern shopping center development has imitated high-end centers in the United States and Canada and to some extent in the United Kingdom and continental Europe. These are centers with costly finishes and upscale fashion and accessory retailing that only the wealthy can afford to patronize. It is only in the second or third wave of development that centers designed to meet the needs of the middle or lower-middle classes become prevalent.

Thanks to medical advances, better hygiene, and improved nutrition, people are living longer, particularly in the North. Although older people do not need the same merchandise that younger people do, they hold most of the well-paying jobs and thus most of the money. Older people spend more on services, including leisure activities, than do the young.

In North America, the United Kingdom, and most of continental Europe, these demographics require a rethinking of the retail offerings in centers. And that is precisely what has been going on. Centers are featuring more and more personal services, along with entertainment and dining, both fast-food and upscale restaurants.

In the South, with a few exceptions, the majority of the population is young — below 25 years of age and, in some cases, below 20. And the South's birthrates continue to soar. Meanwhile, birthrates in the North have fallen, in some cases below the replacement level. The North, therefore, needs to import workers, and these workers will be mainly from the South. However, many immigrants will come from distinctly different backgrounds than those of the dwindling majority groups in the North.

CENTER DEVELOPMENT AROUND THE WORLD

Shopping centers move into countries in waves. Typically, the first wave is closely imitative of successful centers in the United States and other industrialized economies and is designed for the affluent. The second wave has food anchors, such as hypermarkets, and is aimed at the ordinary people in the capital cities. The third wave is a combination of the first two, with centers located in provincial capitals and other major cities. Most centers being built in the world today appear to be urban, not suburban.

A whirlwind trip around the globe reveals the following levels of shopping center development in a sampling of geographic areas.

In the United States and Canada, the building phase of the shopping center business is over. Future construction of new centers will bc slight relative to the building that took place during the past half century. What construction there is involves freestanding stores, and any future construction will involve expansion and refurbishment of existing centers much more than new projects.

Mexico, Central America and the northern part of South America hold enormous potential. The few centers that exist are of the first-generation variety, that is, imitations of North American centers aimed largely at the wealthy.

The southern region of South America — Brazil, Argentina, Paraguay, Uruguay, and Chile — presents a more varied picture. These countries have, relatively speaking, more solid economies than in the past, which are less subject to hyperinflation crises and enjoy more stable, democratically elected governments. In these markets, shopping centers are in several phases of development simultaneously. First-generation centers in urban areas are aimed at the more affluent, while hypermarket-based centers, also in urban locations, are designed more with the general populace in mind. Some special attention is being paid to siting centers near transportation facilities, as has occurred in a few instances with train and bus stations in the United States and appears to be in process for major airports.

Except for Puerto Rico, the Caribbean area has few centers of any size. What the future holds is probably more along the lines of mass merchandising for the local population and specialized shops and centers for visitors.

For the moment, in terms of modern shopping centers, Africa means South Africa. The rest of the continent, except for the North African nations on the Mediterranean, are a long way from the economic level that can support organized retailing of the kind needed to make centers work.

The wealth of the Gulf States and other oil-rich nations of the Middle East makes almost anything possible. Shopping centers have flourished for some time in several locations; others are under development.

Shopping center development in Asia is well advanced. In general, the vertical shopping center is likely to continue to be widely used, although perhaps not so rigidly in countries where land is available and affordable. Japan resembles the United States, Canada, and Northern Europe in the maturity of its retailing. Singapore and Hong Kong are similarly mature in their development and operation of centers. Malaysia, Indonesia and Thailand are all undergoing massive expansion programs featuring megacenters like those pioneered in the Philippines, but on an even larger scale.

China remains a case apart, of course, with major differences between the southern provinces and the capital versus the rest of that vast nation. South Korea has a number of significant projects but remains somewhat apart from the rest of Asia, as does Vietnam. India holds great promise.

However, there is a real question if bigger and more means better. Westerners confronted with the pace and scale of development in Asia are typically awed and skeptical that the space being built will ever be put to good use. Asians, particularly those involved in building these centers, respond that the western eye misses the rapidly growing middle class whose prosperity, indeed affluence, will make all the residential, hotel, and retail development understandable.

BUILDING A FOUNDATION FOR DIALOGUE

Having a substantial library of constructed retail projects provides the opportunity to extract from them lessons of successes, failures, and near misses that can substantially improve the opportunities for success in future shopping centers. These success stories exist not as projects themselves, but as elements of projects, as well as their specific details, which can be extracted and applied to future projects. These elements act as building blocks used to construct a common language that the international shopping center community can apply. This language can transcend borders and the divergent customs and business relationships around the world. These cultural differences are most clearly demonstrated in comparing North American and Asian center plans.

The North American regional shopping center is generally built on a large piece of land 80 acres (32 hectares) or more, on one or two levels, and is frequently up to 1,200 feet (365 meters) in length. It is characterized by ample skylight, open vistas from floor to floor, department stores interspersed with other stores about 300 feet (90 meters) apart, ground-floor lease depths of 90 feet (27 meters), second-floor lease depths of 60-75 feet (18-23 meters) and shop widths of varying dimensions. Servicing is generally from the rear so as to maintain a positive image and to provide code-required exit corridors. Mall walkway widths on lower levels are generally in the range of 30 feet (9 meters), while the upper-level walkways do not exceed 15 feet (4.5 meters). Typical mall building cross-sections allow for

A

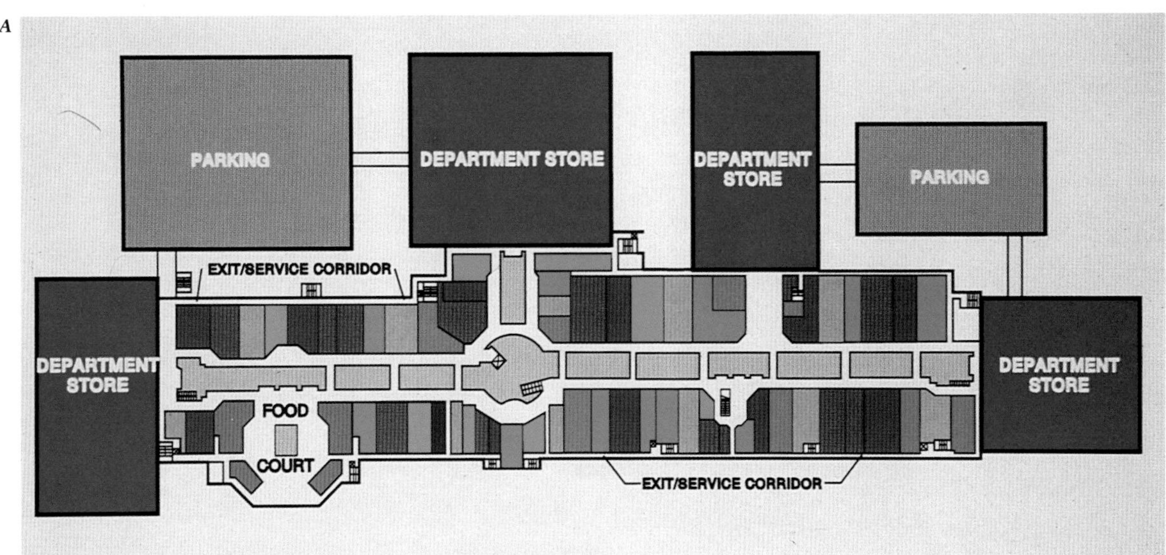

B

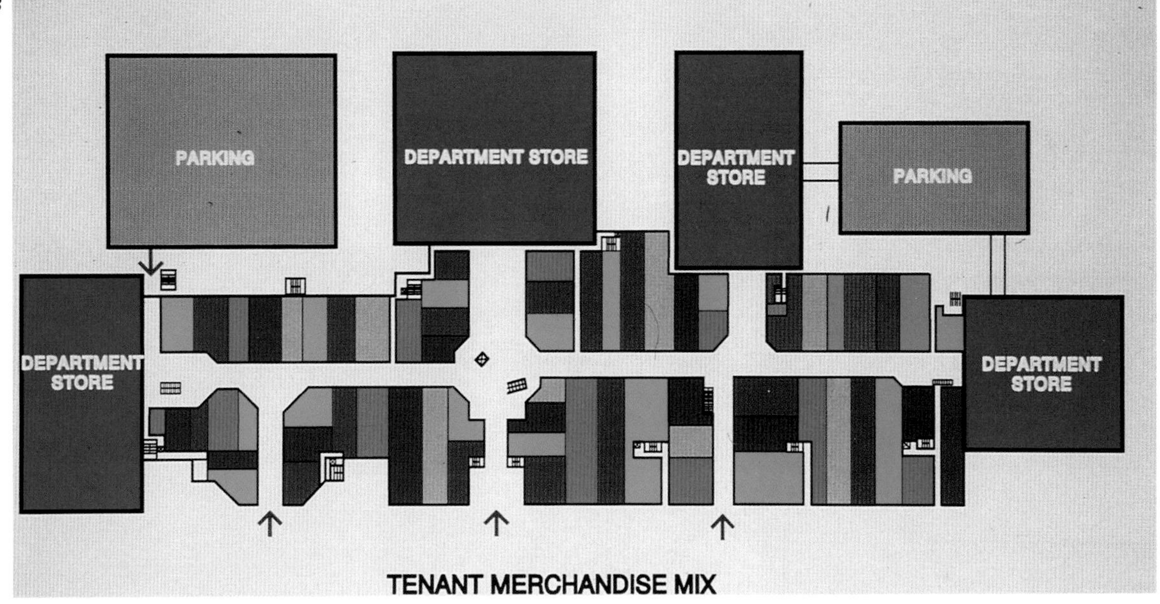

A. *Arden Fair Sacramento, California*

B. *Arden Fair Sacramento, California*

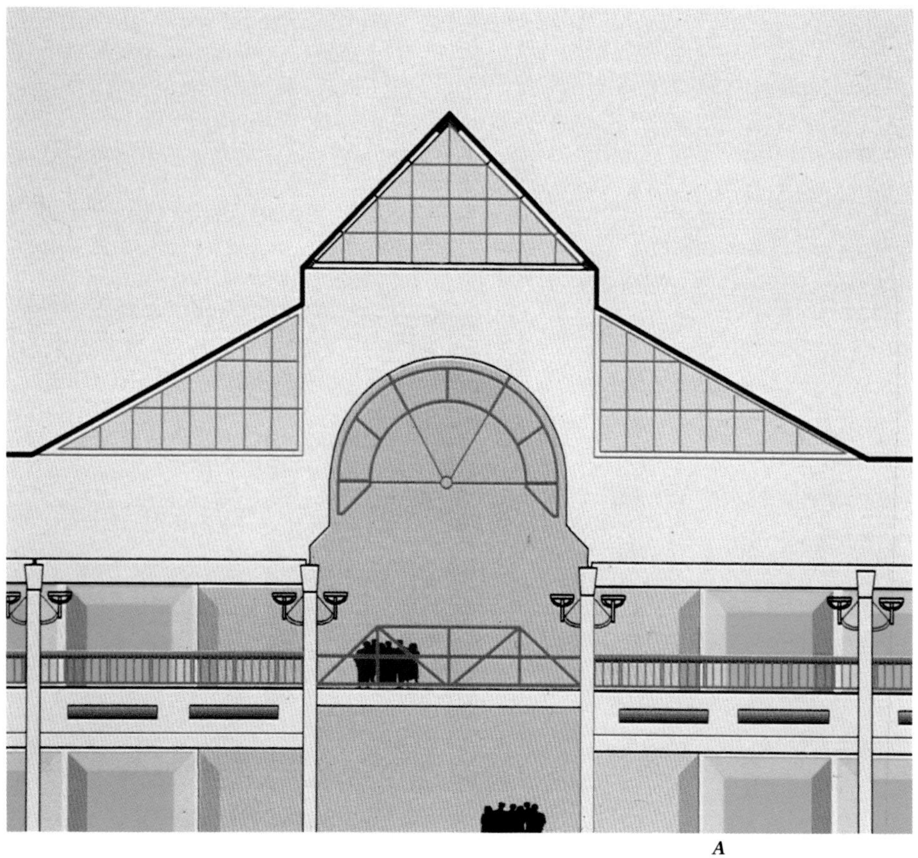

A

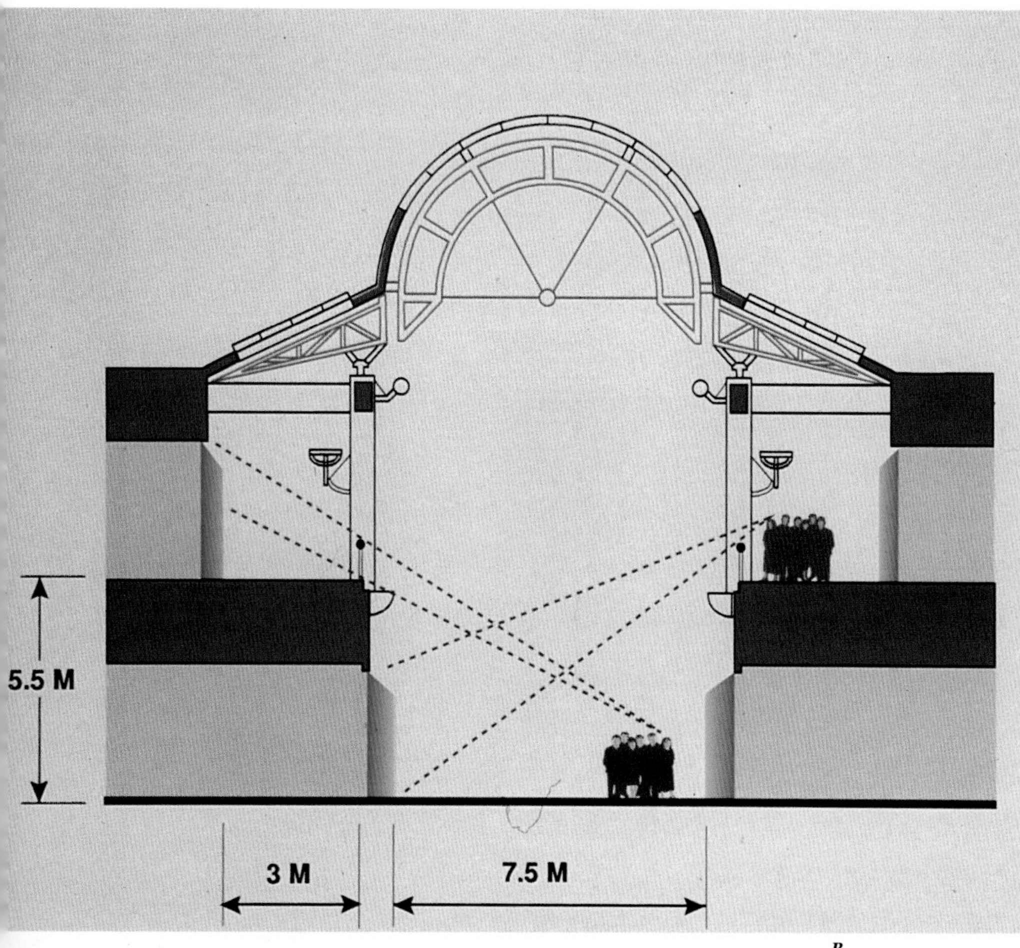

B

optimal visibility between shopping levels to maximize shop front exposure.

The typical shopper in a North American center is an individual who wishes to get in and out as quickly as possible and therefore demands abundant and readily available parking. The prototypical American mall has not served the anticipated social purposes customarily assigned to the town square or plaza. They neither provide a natural social venue, nor serve as a place for family activities. They are seen more as an amenity supporting commercial targets, which are surgically approached for specific items, rather than casually as one would encounter on a stroll down Main Street.

By contrast, the Asian center is on a tight urban site, is much more compact, and often rises six or more levels with a single central focal space. Lease depths are much shallower, ranging from 3 to 9 meters (10 to 30 feet). Nearly all servicing is through the front of the shop because codes generally do not require exiting from the rear. Responsive to specific cultural nuances, mall widths are more generous than the North American prototype, as extended families or other large clusters of people often shop together. This shopping pattern also affects the general merchandise mix, which is far less

A. *Arden Fair Sacramento, California*

B. *Arden Fair Sacramento, California*

C. *Taman Anggrek Jakarta, Indonesia (Opposite)*

D. *Taman Anggrek Jakarta, Indonesia (Opposite)*

sophisticated, due to the infancy of the formal retail industry in Asia. Often building cross-sections do not give floor to floor visibility for shop fronts, except in central atrium spaces.

In areas particularly close to the equator, sunlight is not a friend and substantially less is allowed to brighten the mall. Few centers can be characterized as being joyful because the artificial decorative lighting, often intended by designers to offset the absence of daylight, is often a casualty of cost reduction during construction. Parking is generally provided at a lower ratio than in the North American prototype. Unusually tight parking standards prevail, with only 60%-75% of the space per car that is allotted in Western centers. And ample room is provided for drivers, waiting areas, car paging facilities, bicycles, motorcycles, and buses. Frequently tandem parking is stacked many cars deep and is also accommodated within driving aisles. With fewer private vehicles, public transportation is a necessity for the Asian center, while it is seen as a nuisance in the West.

In multi-level centers, often over six levels, merchandising zones of like products seem more realistic than the method of dispersed merchandising used in the West. Therefore, the benefit of inducing customers to browse in nearby shops during their comparison shopping for similar items must be augmented by other merchandising strategies.

The Asian center accommodates the family. Often, with three generations of shoppers within the family, there is a requirement for entertainment for the young and energetic crowd, serious comparison shopping for the middle generation, and relaxation and people-watching activities for the elder generation.

The customs by which business itself is conducted between landlord and tenant, between wholesaler and retailer, between tenant and customer, is as different from country to country as night is from day. The manner in which rents are paid in the North American center has a specific relationship to the sales performance of the merchant. After the merchant has paid a base rent, the more successful and profitable the merchant, the higher the ultimate percentage rent a developer will receive. Accordingly, the developer has a vested interest in creating and maintaining a retail environment which encourages greater shopping activity and frequency of occurrence. This business relationship causes the landlord to develop sophisticated programs for security, property management, maintenance, promotions, and public relations. In those parts of the world where sales are not recorded, or where income taxes are not stringently enforced, a partnership relationship between landlord and tenant would depend on a level of candor often in conflict with many cultures' proclivity toward individual privacy.

C

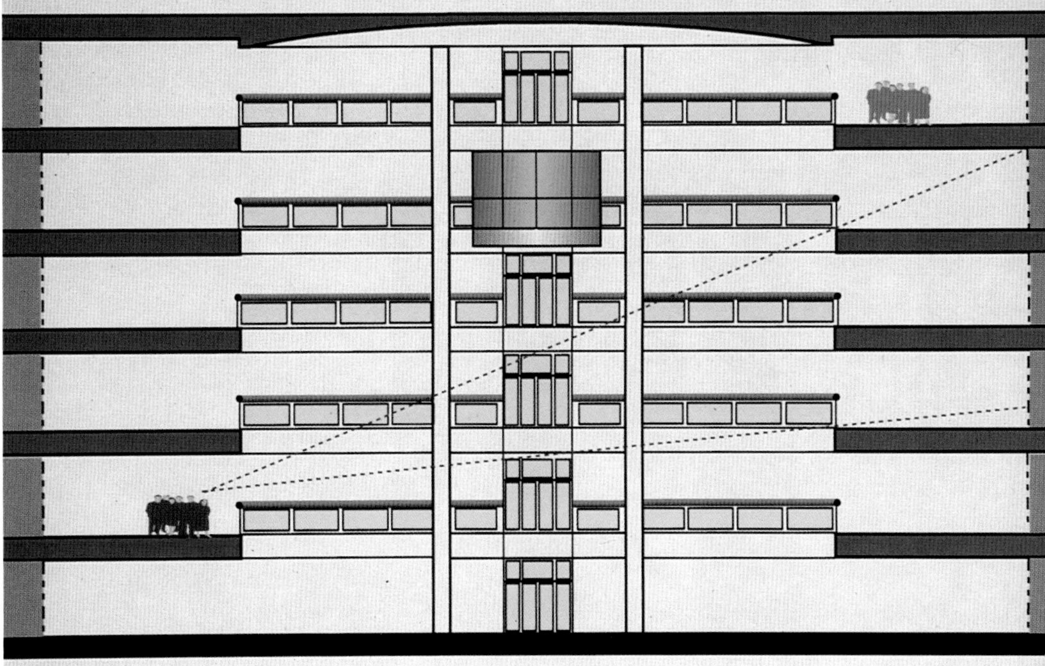

D

In North America nearly every tenant shop has its own toilet facilities available for sales staff and occasionally for customers. As this is not usually the case in Asia, shops are forced to close when proprietors go to use remote restrooms. Customers are often left uninformed as to when the proprietor may return. Although the labor pool in Asia is relatively inexpensive, and often multiple salespeople attend in each shop, they often eat their lunch at the selling counter, which is seen as positive in both the business and social sense. This practice is almost never seen in North American shopping centers and is usually forbidden by employers.

In the United States at least two urban centers sought — each in its own way — to imitate the Asian vertical approach. They failed even though the merchandise they offered was attractive and similar to that available at nearby horizontal centers. At one level, this situation is puzzling because before the advent of shopping centers the major form of retailing in the United States was freestanding department stores. Most of these were rectangular or square, but all were multi-level and usually had elevators on one side of the building, which were later augmented or replaced by escalators in the center. North American shoppers were accustomed to this type of verticality, often encompassing over five levels. They accepted it then; they accept it today in those same department stores, which serve as anchors to larger retail complexes.

So why did these vertical centers fail? Why have other attempts at vertical centers on tight sites not worked? The main reason is that department stores were and are comprised of "departments," which are predictable destinations of their own. Specific merchandise collections, such as housewares, evening wear, or ready to wear women's casuals, draw customers vertically to these merchandise collections, much as shopping center stores draw customers horizontally. There was also the absence of clear lines of sight and direct traffic patterns that department store merchants had long ago perfected. Above all else is a reason that is customer related. The North American shopper has convenient horizontal format options and does not need to navigate the more confusing vertical alternatives. In contrast, the enormous masses of people patronizing Asian centers physically forces customers to upper levels, which is decidedly not the case in the United States.

In spite of all these differences between the North American shopping center and others around the world, there still exists the instinct to review the North American prototype and to apply it to meet the retailing demand around the world. And yet, this prototype cannot be specifically applied without substantial modification. Just as poetry is most difficult to precisely translate from language to language and culture to culture, so it is with specific building types.

A. *Taman Anggrek Jakarta, Indonesia*

B. *Taman Anggrek Jakarta, Indonesia*

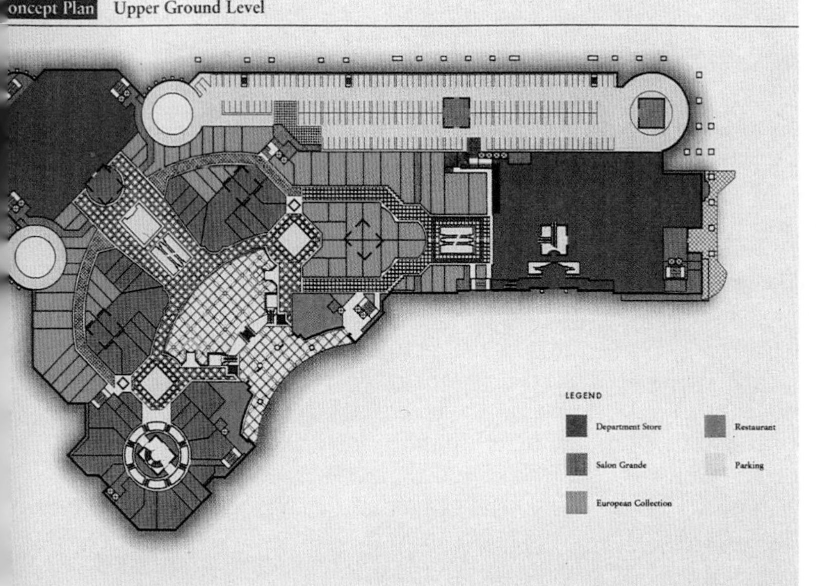

A

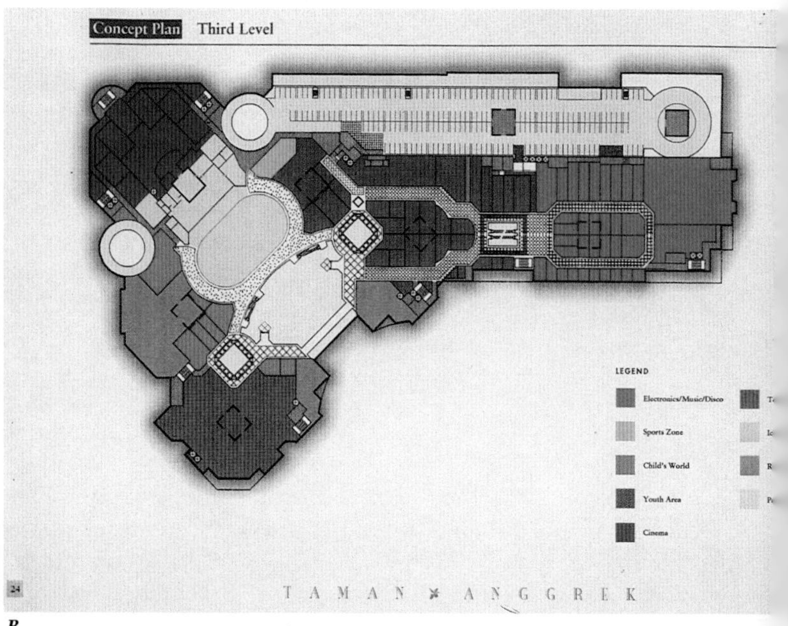

B

DETAILS THAT TRAVEL WELL

Although overall shopping center concepts may not travel well (or at all), many of their programmatic elements and details do. These pieces can be thought of as the "nouns, adjectives, and verbs" of the "language" of the regional shopping center. Broken apart and reassembled they can apply to new concepts that will be developed to transcend borders. What follows is a rundown of those details that have been successfully adapted or have helped make completely new concepts suitable for a given country or location.

A

B

C

D

E

F

A. *The Shops at Liberty Place Philadelphia, Pennsylvania*

B. *Universal CityWalk Universal City, California*

C. *Sherman Oaks Galleria Sherman Oaks, California*

D. *Phipps Plaza Atlanta, Georgia*

E. *The Gallery at Harborplace Baltimore, Maryland*

F. *Arden Fair Sacramento, California*

ENTRANCES

If the eyes are windows to the soul, so are entrances reflections of a center's energy. Beyond being the first and last impression of the shopping center experience, entrance elements can reflect the mall interior architecture and, as a salient symbol, can convey the quality of the building and the merchants. In the end they can function as a logo identity of the shopping center. In those countries where there is a higher incidence of chauffeured personal vehicles or even public transit, the entrance serves as the project foyer and is called upon to handle larger numbers of people. This is all the more reason for a formidable entrance.

A. *Kaahumanu Center Kahului, Maui, Hawaii*

B. *The Mall at Green Hills Nashville, Tennessee (Opposite)*

A

Photo courtesy David Franzen © 1995

THE MALL AT
Green Hills

A

A. *North Point Mall Alpharetta, Georgia*

B. *The Galleria Morley Perth, Australia*

C. *Market Square at Arden Fair Sacramento, California (Opposite)*

B

B

PAVING

As the surface underfoot, the paving is an element that every customer touches. As it is also the most visible and memorable surface, it represents the greatest opportunity for an owner to convey its intentions as to the quality of the shopping center. More than just the critical issues of maintenance and performance need to be addressed. The paved area represents a palette that can establish the foundation for the overall ambiance of a shopping center. The opportunities for individuality are endless. But, increasingly, the character of the shopping experience will be uniquely defined for each center by this critical plane, as well as the surface overhead.

A

A. *Phipps Plaza*
Atlanta, Georgia

B. *Fort Worth Town Center*
Fort Worth, Texas
(Opposite)

C

A

B

A. *Plaza del Atlantico Arecibo, Puerto Rico (Opposite)*

B. *Sherman Oaks Galleria Sherman Oaks, California (Opposite)*

C. *The Plaza at King of Prussia King of Prussia, Pennsylvania*

D. *Saint Louis Galleria St. Louis, Missouri*

C

D

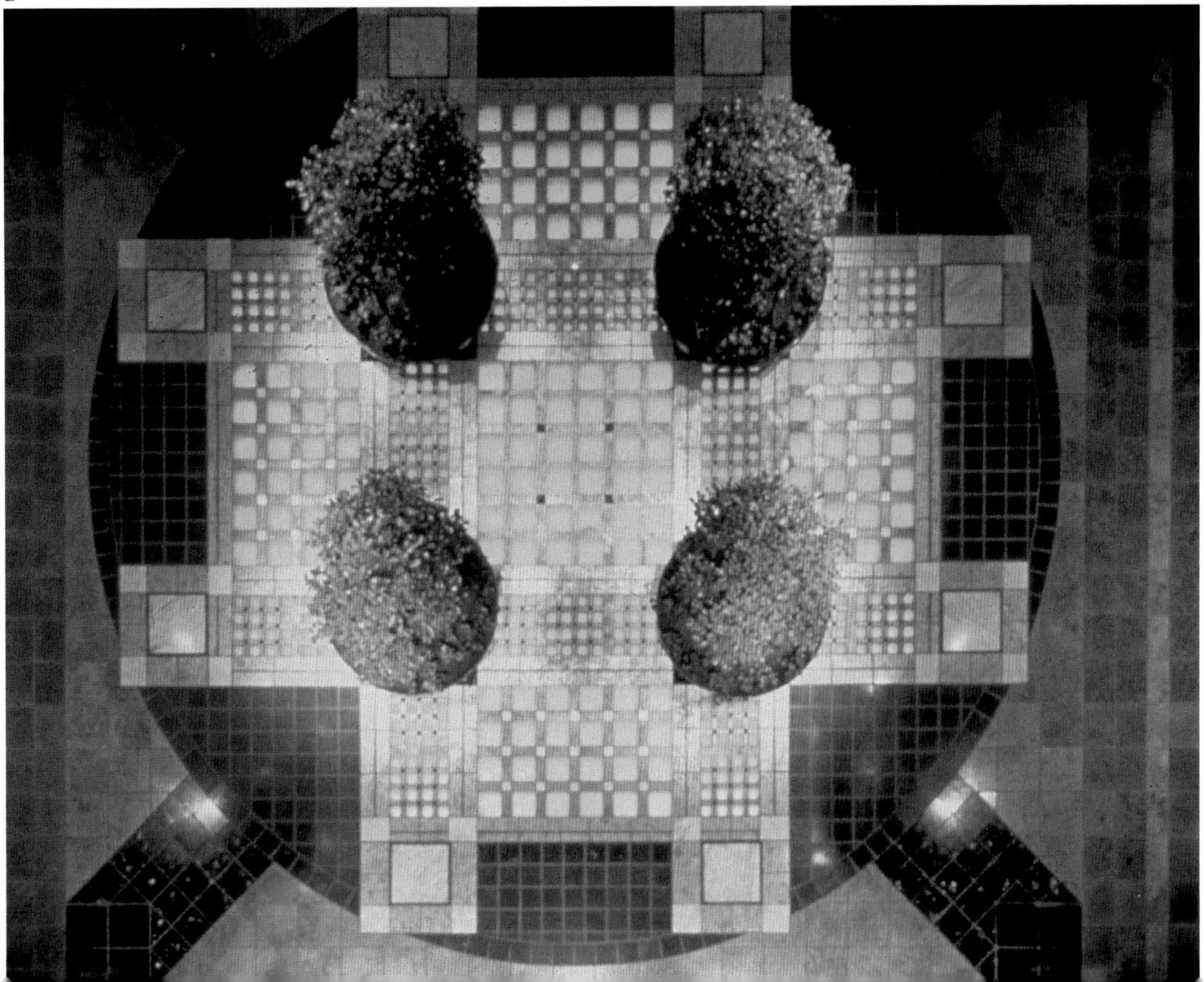

HANDRAILS

Apart from defining the path of movement and providing security, the handrail, like a ribbon of light, reflects the quality of a center through its cleanliness and refinement. Those elements that customers touch convey tactile messages that can reinforce the larger concept. Visibility of shops on upper levels can be facilitated or encumbered by the design of the handrail. Mies van der Rohe, the German-born American architect, once wrote that "God is in the details." If this is true, in a shopping center it is in the handrail where this is most evident.

A

A. *The Natick Mall Natick, Massachusetts*

B. *Tower Place Cincinnati, Ohio*

C. *Sportsgirl Centre Melbourne, Australia (Opposite)*

B

c

B

C

A. *Phipps Plaza Atlanta, Georgia (Opposite)*

B. *Valencia Town Center Valencia, California*

C. *Arden Fair Sacramento, California*

STAIRS

Climbing through space need not be a chore. It can be made to feel like a place of grand arrival that will help put the customer into a shopping-oriented frame of mind. Utilitarian stairs denote work; something the shopper resents. But stairs that somehow engage the customer are an attraction that contributes to the overall experience.

A. *The Mall at Rockingham Park Salem, New Hampshire*

B. *Sportsgirl Centre Melbourne, Australia (Opposite)*

A

Photo courtesy Peter Vanderwalker Photography.

B

A

A. *Bellevue Square Bellevue, Washington*

B. *Houston Town & Country Mall Houston, Texas (Opposite)*

ESCALATORS

These "staircases" moving through space must be located so as to reinforce the overall circulation plan for a shopping center. Properly situated, they can work in concert with the merchandising plan, both formal and informal. As one has a captive audience for the duration of the ride, extraordinary opportunities exist for promotional displays and activities. The additional expense of wider treads helps make escalators more friendly, especially to shoppers with young children or the elderly.

A

A. *The Natick Mall Natick, Massachusetts*

B. *Mall at 163rd Street North Miami Beach, Florida (Opposite)*

C. *Sherway Gardens Etobicoke, Ontario Canada (Opposite)*

B

C

ELEVATORS

As the word "entertainment" has found its way into the vocabulary of retail architecture, the elevators have become a primary mechanism of reinforcing that spirit. Glass enclosed, oversized elevator platforms appear user-friendly to customers and allow patrons with baby carriages or in wheelchairs to freely access a center without imposing on other customers. Often designed as more playful objects, colorful and decoratively lit, elevators themselves have become places from which and in which to promote the excitement of a center.

A

B

A. *Arden Fair Sacramento, California*

B. *Deerbrook Mall Houston, Texas*

C. *The Plaza at King of Prussia King of Prussia, Pennsylvania (Opposite)*

C

BALCONIES

Like an opera box, balconies add a level of richness to the overall design of a retail mall. In addition, they provide a place of repose amid the bustle of a shopping center, where customers can sit, rest and passively observe the ongoing activity in the center. They can be conveniently located intermittently along a mall's thoroughfare without causing undue disruption to customer circulation. And this absolves the developer from the need to provide large expanded areas for relaxation.

A. *The Mall at Green Hills Nashville, Tennessee*

B. *Arden Fair Sacramento, California (Opposite)*

A

B

BRIDGES

Over the years, the shopping center has evolved to allow maximum visibility of merchant storefronts between shopping levels. Narrower bridges have replaced wide and heavy platforms to encourage merchant success and are strategically located to provide adequate cross-mall circulation. Now, lighter bridge structures, which extend architectural details overhead, create even less cumbersome elements. These lighter bridges, which customers walk through, create a zone of more personal space and can reinforce the overall architectural identity of each individual shopping center.

A

B

C

A. *The Gallery at Harborplace Baltimore, Maryland (Opposite)*

B. *Arden Fair Sacramento, California (Opposite)*

C. *The Mall at Green Hills Nashville, Tennessee*

SKYLIGHTS

No single element of a shopping center contributes greater definition to a space than its roof structure and skylight. Natural light defines space and creates a presence and quality that cannot be replicated through artificial means. Yet every region of the world is affected differently by its relationship to the solar environment. Developers of centers close to the equator seem less convinced than their counterparts elsewhere of the benefits of natural light. Proximity to the equator, therefore, causes special challenges for designers seeking to bring a sense of uniqueness and joy to each center they design.

A. *The Natick Mall Natick, Massachusetts*

B. *Phipps Plaza Atlanta, Georgia (Opposite)*

A

B

A

B

A. *Tower Place Cincinnati, Ohio (Opposite)*

B. *The Mall at Green Hills Nashville, Tennessee (Opposite)*

C. *The Galleria Morley Perth, Australia*

D. *The Plaza at King of Prussia King of Prussia, Pennsylvania*

E. *Kaahumanu Center Kahului, Maui, Hawaii*

C

D

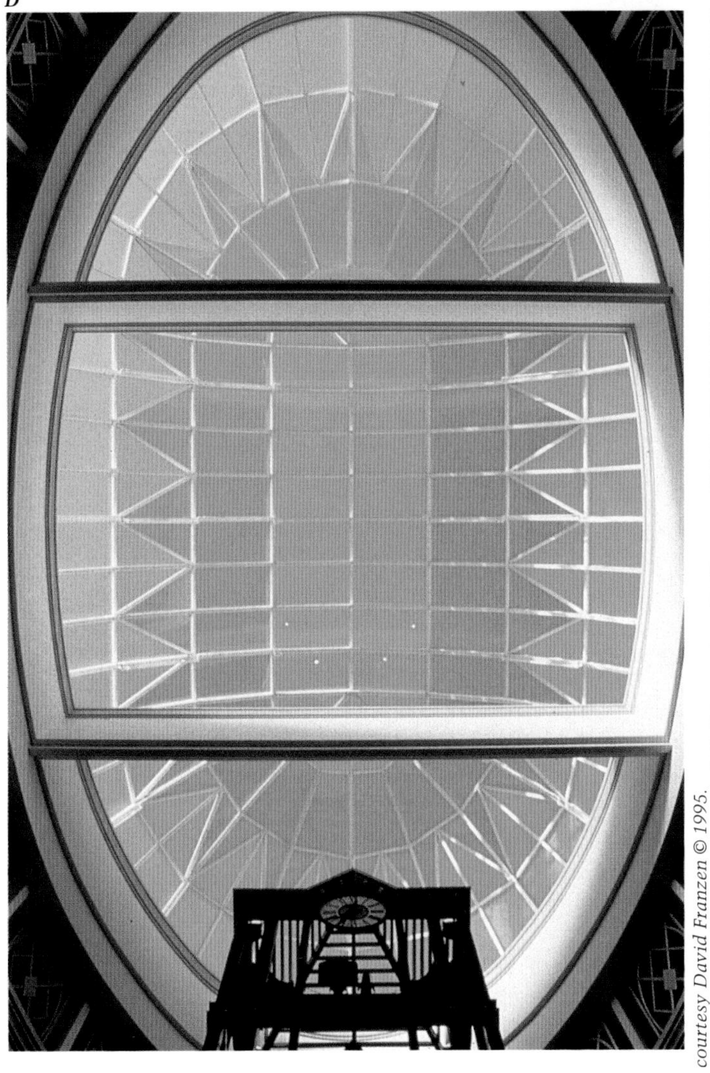

Photo courtesy David Franzen © 1995.

E

SPECIALTY LIGHTING

While providing the ambient light for each shopping center, specialty lighting also creates an air of individuality that reinforces the architecture and allows it to be understood with the greatest and most dramatic impact. This is the necessary and serious lighting that satisfies a center's basic illumination needs. But it also brings spaces alive and reinforces their essential character.

A *Photo courtesy David Franzen © 1995.*

B

C

D

A. *Kaahumanu Center Kahului, Maui, Hawaii (Opposite)*

B. *The Gallery at Harborplace Baltimore, Maryland (Opposite)*

C. *Arden Fair Sacramento, California*

D. *Plaza Rio Hondo Bayamon, Puerto Rico*

A

B

A. *The Mall at Green Hills Nashville, Tennessee*

B. *Arden Fair Sacramento, California*

C. *Tower Place Cincinnati, Ohio (Opposite)*

c

DECORATIVE LIGHTING

In the absence of sunlight, decorative lighting acts as a counterpoint to a space and injects a sense of fantasy into the shopping experience. It enriches a shopping center and creates a special aura in a manner similar to what cufflinks bring to suits and jewelry brings to dresses. Often playful and sometimes animated, it works psychologically to establish interest and joy.

A. *Lincolnwood Town Center Lincolnwood, Illinois*

B. *Pembroke Lakes Mall Pembroke Pines, Florida (Opposite)*

A

Babbage's

A

A. *The Mall at Rockingham Park Salem, New Hampshire*

B. *Chadstone Chadstone, Australia (Opposite)*

B

KIOSKS

In earlier generations of shopping centers, kiosks appeared temporary in nature, as did the merchants who occupied them. That transient message was often in conflict with the seriousness of an overall fashion theme. Now, by maintaining absolute control over the design of kiosks, a center can help its least sophisticated tenants, in the most prominent locations, to become positive contributors to the center. The kiosks can provide a more intimate scale to a center, more akin to streetscape furnishings. At the same time their festive marketplace imagery adds a level of spontaneity that complements more serious in-line shops.

A

A. *Spring Hill Mall West Dundee, Illinois (Opposite)*

B. *Mall of America Bloomington, Minnesota*

B

ARCHITECTURAL LANDSCAPE

In many communities, the unavailability of appropriate landscape, the spatial demands, the costs of maintenance, or the absence of a natural light source precludes the use of specimen trees within shopping center complexes. In such situations, or when a more urban character is desired, the inclusion of highly architectural landscape elements is often more appropriate. There is a large vocabulary of garden-related elements, including trellises, arbors, column trees, pot rails, and landscape troughs that can be introduced to create a highly sophisticated landscape presence, utilizing easily maintainable or replaceable plant materials.

A

B

A. *Arden Fair Sacramento, California (Opposite)*

B. *The Natick Mall Natick, Massachusetts (Opposite)*

C. *Lincolnwood Town Center Lincolnwood, Illinois*

D. *Lincolnwood Town Center Lincolnwood, Illinois*

C

D

LANDSCAPE

In venues where a tradition of landscape maintenance exists, and landscape specimens are plentiful, more conventional approaches to landscape provide soft, quiet places that contrast with the high energy focus of retail complexes. Here, conventional plantings of trees, shrubs, and colorful flowers provide a welcome respite from and counterpoint to retail activity. Trees are often planted directly in the ground, with grates or under plantings, or in oversized pots, where space allows.

A. *The Plaza at King of Prussia*
King of Prussia, Pennsylvania

B. *Lincolnwood Town Center*
Lincolnwood, Illinois

C. *Arden Fair*
Sacramento, California
(Opposite)

A

B

C

FOUNTAINS

Water is a design feature common to all cultures. Fountains may be for visual or audio impact, can be traditional in form, or incorporated as a work of art, and may be passive or interactive. While the latter poses a maintenance and safety problem, interactive fountains have become exceptionally popular with younger people and parents with children, who appreciate their entertainment value. However applied, fountains are visually most popular with customers of all ages.

A

B

A. *The Gallery at Harborplace Baltimore, Maryland (Opposite)*

B. *Tower Place Cincinnati, Ohio*

C. *Atrium Court Fashion Island Newport Beach, California*

C

AMENITIES

The furnishings in malls are immediately translatable from culture to culture. While styles and types of benches and chairs do bear local nuances, they are generically a part of life for all of us. Amenities, which include backed and backless benches, chairs, trash receptacles, ash trays, drinking fountains, telephones and bicycle racks, are often crafted locally, based on more expensive designs that could be imported. These copies frequently underperform those which have been manufactured to meet stringent performance specifications, so the production and testing of alternate elements should be reviewed carefully.

A

A. *Arden Fair Sacramento, California (Opposite)*

B. *The Mall at Green Hills Nashville, Tennessee*

B

ARTWORK

Much more common in North America than in other regions, art has found its place as a cultural asset with lasting community value. The public relations benefit from sponsoring and implementing an arts program, and the extended benefit of outreach programs that frequently engage primary and secondary schools, build a two-way commitment within a community. That relationship helps position a center as specifically tailored to, and reflective of, the community it serves. In some cases it is possible to rotate an arts program from center to center. However, this is ill-advised if the art was specifically commissioned for a unique space.

A

A. *Darling Harbourside Sidney, Australia (Opposite)*

B. *Valencia Town Center Valencia, California.*

C. *Tower Place Cincinnati, Ohio*

B

C

A

A. *Arden Fair Sacramento, California*

B. *Deerbrook Mall Houston, Texas (Opposite)*

B

SIGNAGE

The highly sophisticated signage systems of Europe, and the playful and artistic approaches of North America, are contributing measurably to the quality of the retailing experience in those venues. Such signage programs are meeting resistance in development projects in less industrialized countries, primarily because of the unexpected cost of design, and more particularly because of limited resources for local fabrication and installation. Despite the difficulties of implanting this element into countries where the support systems for fabrication are unavailable, adequate signage does have significant bearing on the success of projects and should not be overlooked.

A

B

C

D

E

A. *Worcester Common Fashion Outlets Worcester, Massachusetts (Opposite)*

B. *Sportsgirl Centre Melbourne, Australia (Opposite)*

C. *The Plaza at King of Prussia King of Prussia, Pennsylvania*

D. *The Mall at Green Hills Nashville, Tennessee*

E. *Liberty Place Philadelphia, Pennsylvania*

ENVIRONMENTAL GRAPHICS

Beyond functional signage systems are the graphic design elements that help to embellish the theme of a center down to the smallest detail. Often, these elements are more playful than informative, more colorful than functional. Yet they form a part of the entertaining vocabulary of a center that is no less important than is landscape or decorative lighting. It is these graphic elements that recall the specific theme of a project, tie it to a specific place, and allow that project to measurably separate itself from its competition in the consumer's eye.

A. *Kendall Town & Country Shopping Center Kendall, Florida*

B. *Triangle Square Costa Mesa, California*

C. *Kaahumanu Center Kahului, Maui, Hawaii (Opposite)*

A

B

Photo courtesy David Franzen © 1995.

C

A

A. The Natick Mall Natick, Massachusetts

B. Lincolnwood Town Center Lincolnwood, Illinois

C. Lincolnwood Town Center Lincolnwood, Illinois (Opposite)

D. The Natick Mall Natick, Massachusetts (Opposite)

B

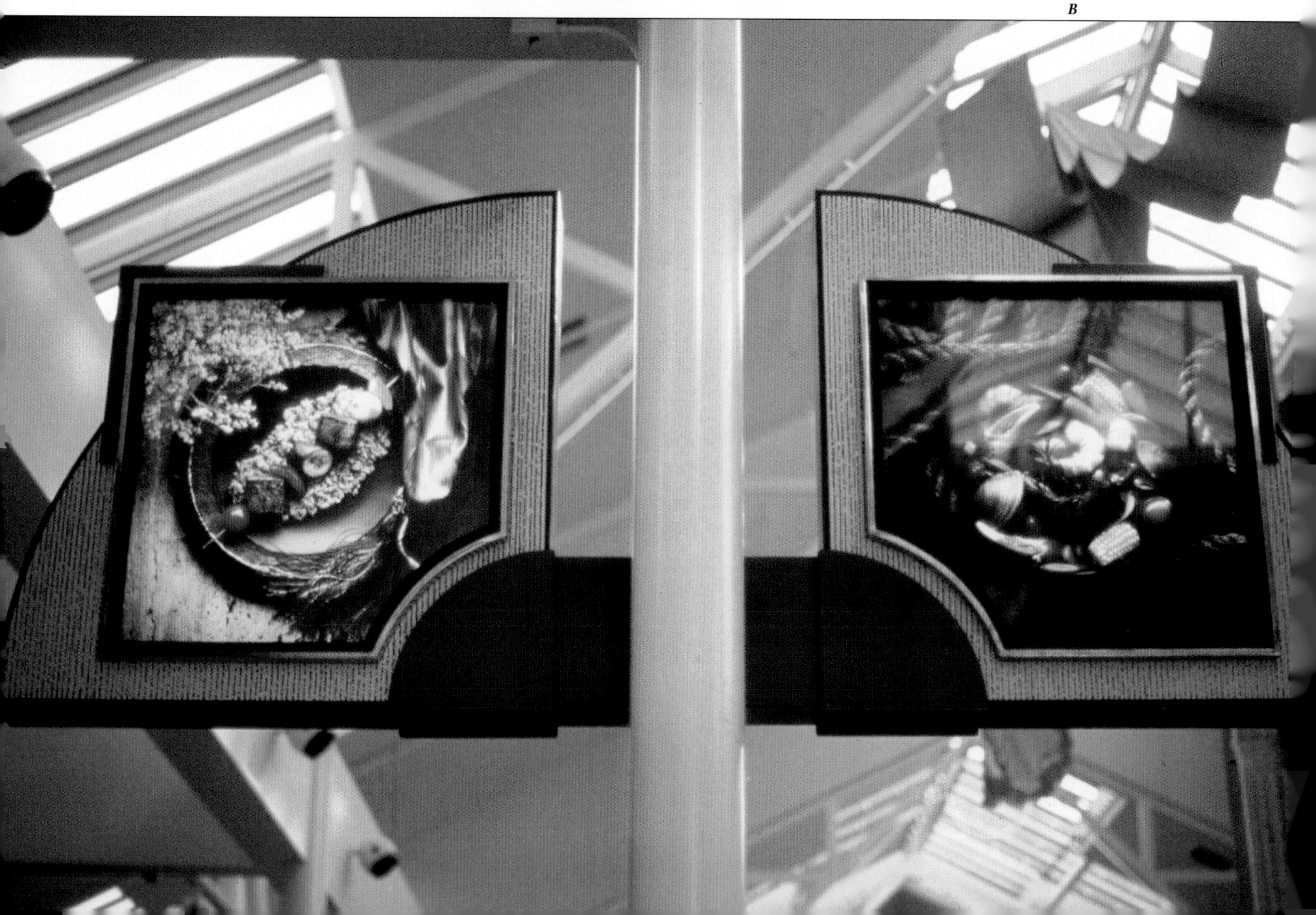

C

D

DIRECTORIES

The graphic design begins with the directories, which not only communicate information to the visitor, but also introduce the theme of the center. Directories should be functional, attractive, flexible, and durable. They are the formal greeting of a center and should not be confusing; they can also provide other useful community or promotional information. Individual pocket directories are often available in such locations.

A. *Manhattan Village Shopping Center Manhattan Beach, California*

B. *Lincolnwood Town Center Lincolnwood, Illinois (Opposite)*

C. *Universal CityWalk Universal City, California (Opposite)*

D. *Saint Louis Galleria St. Louis, Missouri (Opposite)*

A

B

C

LEVEL
2
BILLIARDS BAR GRILL
UP THE ESCALATOR
WIZARDZ
BILLIARDS BAR GRILL
UP THE ESCALATOR
WIZARDZ

D

GALLERIA

OTHER ITEMS

There are a myriad of interactive elements and architectural details, from cornices to canopies, tree grates to flagpoles, which combine to create a richness of ambiance and an individual identity for each center. Many designs are derivative from the local culture and help to position a retail property comfortably within the context of its surrounding community. The very best shopping centers create "a sense of place" that fixes that center in the customer's mind as a special, specific place. Properly considered, these elements combine to define a shopping environment that will sustain itself through time as new energetic merchants replace departing ones.

A

A. *Hamilton Eaton Centre Hamilton, Ontario Canada*

B. *The Plaza at King of Prussia King of Prussia, Pennsylvania (Opposite)*

A

B

C

A. *The Mall at Green Hills*
Nashville, Tennessee

B. *The Plaza at King of Prussia*
King of Prussia, Pennsylvania

C. *Kaahumanu Center*
Kahului, Maui, Hawaii

D. *The Shops at Liberty Place*
Philadelphia, Pennsylvania
(Opposite)

E. *Phipps Plaza*
Atlanta, Georgia
(Opposite)

F. *Hamilton Eaton Centre*
Hamilton, Ontario Canada
(Opposite)

Photo courtesy David Franzen © 1995.

D

E

F

A

B

A. *Tower Place Cincinnati, Ohio*

B. *Arden Fair Sacramento, California*

CENTER CONCEPTS AND FORMATS

These elements then, form the parts of speech of a common language of shopping centers. By themselves, these elements convey little or no meaning. They are just like words. However, put together in ways sensitive to the local business and social culture, they ask questions, make statements, and command action. One of the most important actions these words must command is to state the purpose of a center, to define and validate its use.

The biggest failure to communicate comes when visitors to one center see a new retail concept and think they understand it, but later discover they have observed only the surface. The building is a shell; it can be rugged like a clam shell, or delicate and refined like a chambered nautilus. Then, to this shell comes the individual retail hermit crab, which makes a home, creates a life, and goes about its work. To understand retail, one must not only understand the shell, but the true nature of what is going on inside. Merchandise, the tenant mix, and the quality of tenant presentation are as critical as the vessel that contains them.

A

B

C

D

E

F

A. *Deerbrook Mall Houston, Texas*

B. *Santa Monica Place Santa Monica, California*

C. *Arden Fair Sacramento, California*

D. *Randhurst Shopping Center Mt. Prospect, Illinois*

E. *Randhurst Shopping Center Mt. Prospect, Illinois*

F. *The Mall at Rockingham Park Salem, New Hampshire*

TENANT STOREFRONT AND SIGNAGE CRITERIA

The appearance that a tenant brings to a shopping center can be compatible with, substantially enhance, or absolutely destroy the overall quality of the shopping center experience. Left to their own devices, tenants' instincts for the facilities that would best promote their own business success could be entirely incompatible with the overall good of the shopping center. Having made a substantial investment in the construction of a well-coordinated shopping environment, the developer must assure that the tenant storefronts are compatible with and contribute positively to the shopping experience.

A major impression of a shopping center comes from the storefronts. They represent 75% of the vertical image of the shopping environment. If properly designed, the full collection of storefronts can be a stimulating asset for the entire center. To capitalize on their potential often requires education and encouragement, particularly in less sophisticated markets. If legislated properly, through a sound tenant criteria manual and an effective process for reviewing tenant storefront designs, they can contribute extraordinary energy and excitement to a shopping environment.

An effective tenant design criteria manual will provide the tenant with an overall introduction to positioning the property in the retail community; a list of representatives on the development team; a definition of tenant design submittals; the review and approval process; code requirements; insurance requirements; a definition of the building's basic engineering systems; specific storefront criteria for projected, nonprojected, and flush storefronts; acceptable storefront/neutral strip details; a vicinity plan; a site plan; retail mall level plans; building cross-sections; mall materials and finishes; acceptable tenant finish materials for storefronts and interiors; tenant lighting criteria; graphics and signage requirements; specific food court design constraints; utilities information covering sanitary, sewer, water service, telecommunication systems, electric service, gas service, and temporary utilities; and construction criteria. In addition, such a manual should clarify developer and tenant responsibilities for storefronts; electrical; heating, ventilation and air-conditioning; plumbing; sprinkler systems; and detailing which party pays for these items and which installs them. Beyond this information, there should be contractor guidelines that affect the behavior of tenants' contractors.

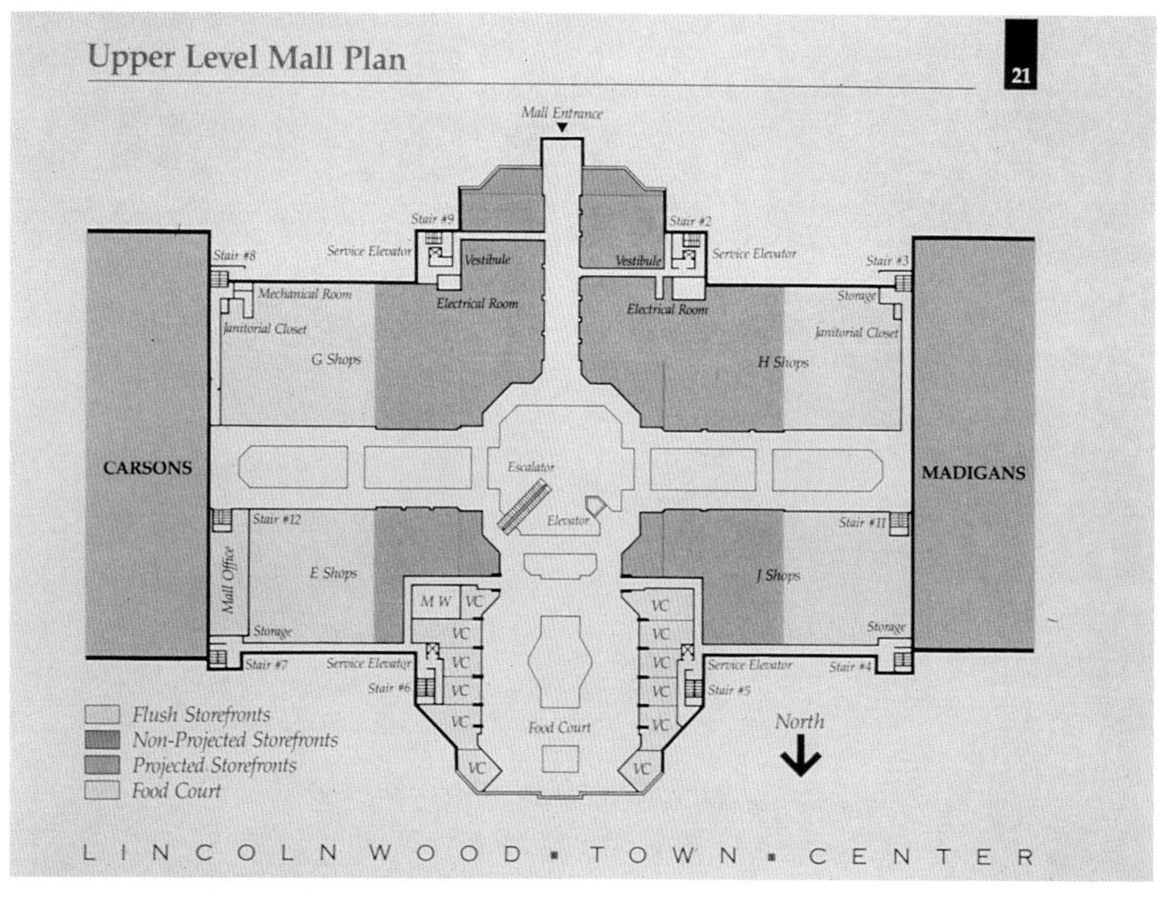

A

A. Lincolnwood Town Center Lincolnwood, Illinois

B. Lincolnwood Town Center Lincolnwood, Illinois (Opposite)

C. Lincolnwood Town Center Lincolnwood, Illinois (Opposite)

D. Lincolnwood Town Center Lincolnwood, Illinois (Opposite)

Skillfully designed, properly incorporated as part of a tenant's lease document, and effectively administered, tenant criteria manuals will initiate a design partnership between the owner and the tenant to assure that the tenant's contribution to the physical environment acts to balance and reinforce the owner's intentions.

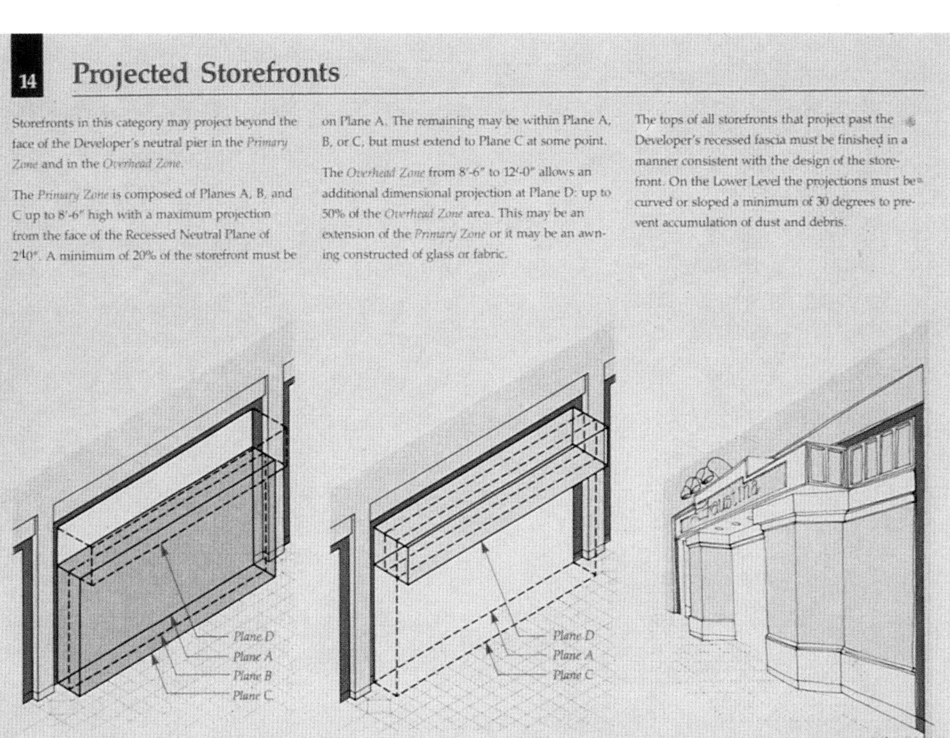

14 Projected Storefronts

Storefronts in this category may project beyond the face of the Developer's neutral pier in the *Primary Zone* and in the *Overhead Zone*.

The *Primary Zone* is composed of Planes A, B, and C up to 8'-6" high with a maximum projection from the face of the Recessed Neutral Plane of 2'-0". A minimum of 20% of the storefront must be on Plane A. The remaining may be within Plane A, B, or C, but must extend to Plane C at some point.

The *Overhead Zone* from 8'-6" to 12'-0" allows an additional dimensional projection at Plane D: up to 50% of the *Overhead Zone* area. This may be an extension of the *Primary Zone* or it may be an awning constructed of glass or fabric.

The tops of all storefronts that project past the Developer's recessed fascia must be finished in a manner consistent with the design of the storefront. On the Lower Level the projections must be curved or sloped a minimum of 30 degrees to prevent accumulation of dust and debris.

L I N C O L N W O O D ▪ T O W N ▪ C E N T E R

B

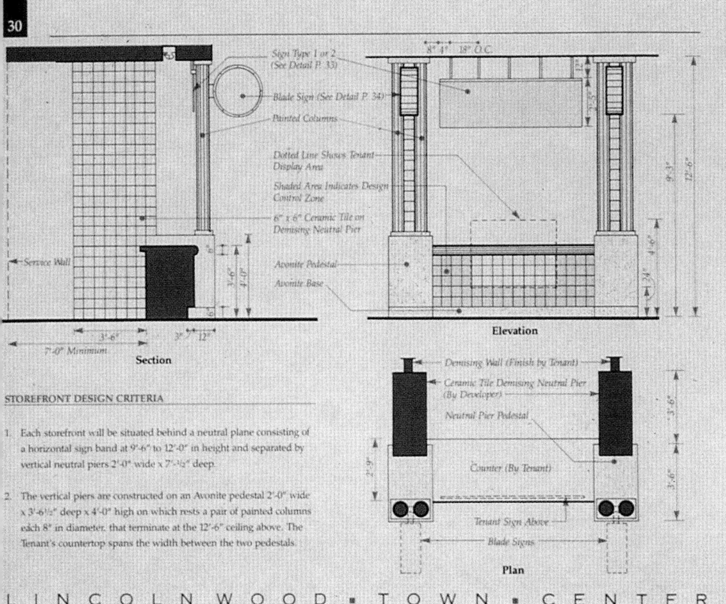

30

STOREFRONT DESIGN CRITERIA

1. Each storefront will be situated behind a neutral plane consisting of a horizontal sign band at 9'-6" to 12'-0" in height and separated by vertical neutral piers 2'-0" wide x 7'-½" deep.

2. The vertical piers are constructed on an Avonite pedestal 2'-0" wide x 3'-6½" deep x 4'-0" high on which rests a pair of painted columns each 8" in diameter, that terminate at the 12'-6" ceiling above. The Tenant's countertop spans the width between the two pedestals.

L I N C O L N W O O D ▪ T O W N ▪ C E N T E R

C

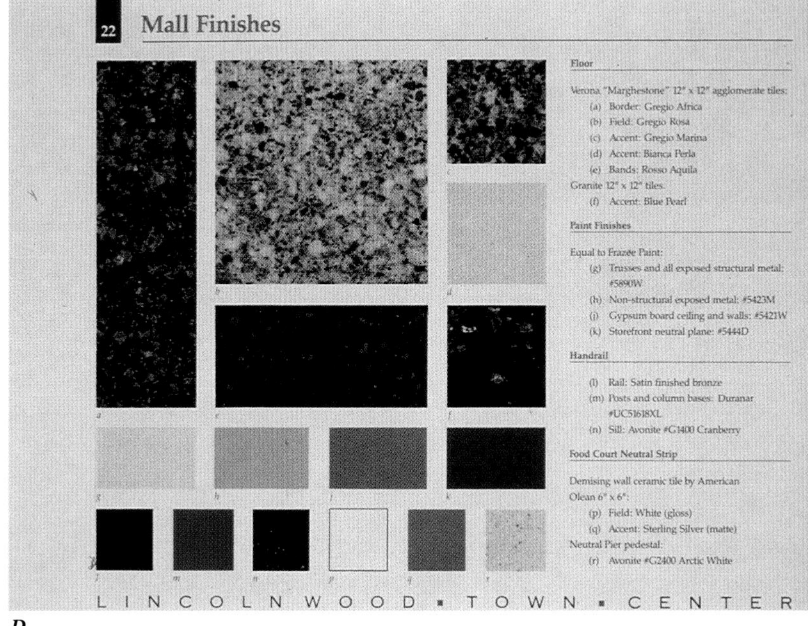

22 Mall Finishes

Floor

Verona "Marghestone" 12" x 12" agglomerate tiles:
- (a) Border: Gregio Africa
- (b) Field: Gregio Rosa
- (c) Accent: Gregio Marina
- (d) Accent: Bianca Perla
- (e) Bands: Rosso Aquila

Granite 12" x 12" tiles:
- (f) Accent: Blue Pearl

Paint Finishes

Equal to Frazee Paint:
- (g) Trusses and all exposed structural metal: #5890W
- (h) Non-structural exposed metal: #5423M
- (j) Gypsum board ceiling and walls: #5421W
- (k) Storefront neutral plane: #5444D

Handrail

- (l) Rail: Satin finished bronze
- (m) Posts and column bases: Duranar #UC51618XL
- (n) Sill: Avonite #G1400 Cranberry

Food Court Neutral Strip

Demising wall ceramic tile by American Olean 6" x 6":
- (p) Field: White (gloss)
- (q) Accent: Sterling Silver (matte)

Neutral Pier pedestal:
- (r) Avonite #G2400 Arctic White

L I N C O L N W O O D ▪ T O W N ▪ C E N T E R

D

STOREFRONTS

Retail storefronts in contemporary shopping centers have their roots in old European cities and the American colonies. Many highly sophisticated, one-of-a-kind storefronts, that were intended to survive generations, are being mimicked superficially in contemporary projects. Standard, off-the-shelf corporate storefronts, which for years conveyed a stagnant image of the retailer, have been replaced by stimulating, designer-aggressive, highly sophisticated, three-dimensional storefront designs. Effective retailers understand that their image begins at the front door. Those companies with multiple outlets have had the opportunity to refine their image consistently. Single location tenants, the "mom and pops" of the retail industry, seem to range from the highly focused and sophisticated, to those who clearly misunderstand the concept of retailing.

A

B

A. *Tower Place*
Cincinnati, Ohio
(Opposite)

B. *Universal CityWalk*
Universal City,
California

PARKING

While downtown automobile congestion helped induce the emergence of the suburban regional shopping center, the automobile itself has become a centerpiece of American culture. Thoughtful and sensitive design of parking lots and parking structures is now mandated by communities in response to vast expanses of cars in unlandscaped parking lots. As the shopping center is placed in urban locations around the world, the need to provide adequate parking in convenient and accessible locations is paramount. As this is a major point of arrival to shopping centers, and bears strongly on the communities surrounding them, the design of these facilities should reflect positively on the overall image of any project.

Typically, parking should be situated so that no retail level is disadvantaged by virtue of its relative inconvenience to parking. The parking lot should be well lit for reasons of customer comfort and security, and adequate signage should provide a clear sense of direction and orientation.

A. *The Mall at Green Hills Nashville, Tennessee*

B. *Gurnee Mills Gurnee, Illinois (Opposite)*

A

OUTLET CENTERS/ FACTORY SURPLUS

As we discuss retail formats that are transplanted successfully, it is also important to understand why it is difficult for prototype formats and concepts of retailing to travel effectively. It is even more important to learn how they can be made adaptable so that they will travel successfully. The discussion below focuses on several key formats and concepts, yet each of them is affected by its presentation and convenience to the shopper.

Sometimes learning how to adapt is not enough. Sometimes what is required is understanding that a business may not be adaptable. For example, Americans and visitors to the United States alike initially did not understand that certain so-called big-box retailers, such as warehouse clubs, are not retail businesses at all. They are wholesale operations based on opportunistic buying, and they make no promises about keeping merchandise in stock. Various office vendors and other kinds of suppliers do sell at retail. But a big part — indeed, often the biggest part — of their clientele buys at wholesale or otherwise in volume, benefiting from volume discounts.

One of the formats that has attracted individual shoppers — and is designed to sell at retail, not wholesale — is the manufacturer or factory outlet center. This concept is also attracting a great deal of interest from the investment community, and such centers in the United States are among the most frequently visited by developers from around the world.

Historically, factory outlets sold surplus merchandise that manufacturers overproduced or merchandise with minor defects. Over time the word "factory" was used less and less and the word "outlet" more and more. Some of the early locations for these factory stores became tourist attractions when "outlets" not directly associated with a factory also opened in the vicinity.

Other districts were deliberately developed, often in old, unused, and therefore inexpensive industrial buildings. Later, outlets were put into relatively inexpensive new buildings at highly trafficked sites distant from the cities and shopping centers where merchandise was sold at regular prices by the manufacturer's retailer clients. Manufacturers did not want to anger their prime retailers by locating their outlet stores near those retailers' own stores. Along with certain mass merchants and discounters, these outlets came to be seen as the low-cost providers of many types of products.

While concern for location is still a big factor, some manufacturers appear to be moving toward the establishment of stores that offer their goods directly to the consumer and are located closer to their department and specialty-store customers. Traditional retailers responded successfully by turning to private-label goods and dropping manufacturer or designer labels completely. Their new approach, in turn, has made it possible for some of the factory outlets to move even closer to the centers of population they tried to avoid in the past.

The heart of the outlet business is merchandise sold at deep discount. For outlets to work, there must be a consistent supply of goods that can be sold at the narrow margins basic to the business. Today some merchandise appears to be manufactured expressly for sale in outlets. Without such an assured supply, success is likely to be uneven or lacking.

B

ANCHORS

First and second wave centers are typically adaptations of large regional or urban centers. Department stores have served as the anchors in North American centers and in some other countries, in part because the first developers of malls in North America were department store companies. Department stores played the anchor role in downtown main-street retailing for many years, so for these stores the transition to anchoring shopping centers was only natural.

However, in some countries there are no department stores and in others, too few exist to create a properly anchored regional shopping environment. Other anchors have had to be found, and new building blocks have had to be created to serve as magnets to draw shoppers. These elements are building blocks which, in the language analogy, are the syntax of the retail center story. Alternatives to the traditional anchors often include supermarkets or hypermarkets, but also include those that follow.

A. *Saks Fifth Avenue Cincinnati, Ohio*

B. *Fort Worth Town Center Fort Worth, Texas (Opposite)*

C. *Valencia Town Center Valencia, California (Opposite)*

A

FOOD COURTS

For the customer, the dining experience should be comfortable and relaxing, and the facilities should be naturally lit and clean. Apart from being uplifting to one's psyche, naturally lit food courts, or those with a view of the adjoining community or landscape, appear to capitalize on the positive aspects of the dining experience. For the owner, it is important to keep tight control over what is generally agreed to be the messiest, hardest-to-discipline aspect of a shopping center's operations. Toilet facilities, with infant changing tables, tray wash facilities, and management offices are often located adjacent and convenient to food courts for reasons of customer satisfaction and security.

B

C

RESTAURANTS

Restaurants are more specific destinations with established clientele. They can be positioned as anchors for a center, as long as they are conveniently located and offer special enough amenities to draw their patrons to the shopping center solely for their use. Often situated adjacent to entrances, they can symbiotically share the energy of a shopping center.

A. *Universal CityWalk Universal City, California*

B. *Marina Marketplace Marina del Rey, California (Opposite)*

C. *Reston Town Center Reston, Virginia (Opposite)*

A

CINEMAS

Traditionally free-standing, cinema clusters with 10 to 20 screens can draw up to 35,000 people per week, adding substantially to the volume of potential shoppers passing through a center. While critics claim that cinemas consume parking spaces that would otherwise go to retail shoppers, they do bring their loyal customers back within the mall on a recurring basis and therefore provide extraordinary exposure to all merchants in the mall. Yet in countries where film distribution monopolies exist, cinemas can substantially underperform their potential and may not achieve their anchoring purpose.

B

C

CHILDREN'S PLAY AREAS

With a large number of hands-on experiential activities, including sports, recreation areas, and children's museums, play areas in shopping centers have become more inventive, more educational, and more thoroughly interactive. Affiliations with product manufacturers, motion picture and cartoon companies, and other performance and athletic organizations can invigorate children's play areas geared to specific community interests.

A

B

A. Al Harthy Complex Muscat, The Sultanate of Oman

B. Mall of America Bloomington, Minnesota

C. Mall of America Bloomington, Minnesota (Opposite)

D. Mall of America Bloomington, Minnesota (Opposite)

INTERACTIVE ENTERTAINMENT

Media arcades have been augmented by elements such as thrill rides and water parks to create special zones of entertainment that are destinations in and of themselves. Because these general uses are so different from the interests of the shopper, one needs to be careful that these zones do not discourage shoppers by creating barriers for the retail shopper to overcome in the course of their comparison shopping experience.

C

D

SOCIAL USE AREAS

Uses that engender passive observation or playful interaction, commonly found in city plazas and urban parks, contribute to the shopping and dining experience as well. These spaces, often unprogrammed, allow elderly shoppers to play chess or checkers, groups to perform tai chi, or to take dancing lessons while others in their party shop more freely. Ice skating rinks, bowling alleys, and roller rinks have often been provided as more active embodiments of social, recreational areas.

A. *Universal CityWalk Universal City, California*

RELAXATION SPACES

Passive park and plaza spaces offer a moment of quiet repose in contrast to the energy of the center. With no particular purpose, they allow shoppers to regain their energy or can be used as a place to meet someone at a certain time.

B. *Valencia Town Center Valencia, California*

B

PROMOTIONAL AREAS

A shopping center has the ability to bring the community together for an overall shopping, dining, entertainment, and recreational experience. It also has an opportunity to be a venue for cultural activities, which may be programmed to a center's evolving clientele and to reinforce seasonal and holiday activities. A promotional area is the center stage for a center and a community and is a space that is completely flexible as well.

A. *Collin Creek*
Plano, Texas

A

BASIC REQUIREMENTS FOR ALL CENTERS

Although nothing is forever, there are a few things that appear to be minimum requirements no matter where in the world centers are located. These form the bedrock of the business and are the fundamentals of the common language of shopping centers.

"OWN, DON'T SELL"

Perhaps the most critical element to long-term success is the ability of the center's owners to control the use of the space, that is, the stores and common areas. While it may not always be possible to finance construction of all the space without selling off some of it or finding innovative financing mechanisms (such as key money in South America), the retail condominium has rarely worked. Recent examples in Europe have produced chaotic situations reminiscent of the gallery form of retailing popular some years ago and still in fashion in some places. Differing operating hours, confusing and inappropriate neighbors in the same retail setting, and quarrels over responsibility for cleaning and maintenance can all be problems. Moreover, the lack of a formal commitment to a common purpose is fatal to the idea of communal free market retailing.

"IT SAYS SO IN THE LEASE"

Control also comes from having comprehensive legal documents that anticipate virtually all issues, all routine operational matters, all responsibilities, and all liabilities. The documents should also give authority to management to act in the event of crisis.

"COMPETITION IS GOOD"

Control through ownership or legal documents makes it possible to promote competition within the same center, something which retailers naturally oppose. As difficult as it is for some merchants to accept, good competition is helpful, and no competition is worse than bad competition. Most successful merchants have achieved their success through the gradual refinement of their product and merchandising, necessitated by a highly competitive marketplace.

PERCENTAGE/ OVERAGE RENTS

In some jurisdictions, custom or law provides only for agreed-to flat rents. Even with built-in periodic upward adjustments based on some notion of inflation, the flat rate arrangement provides little incentive for the landlord to continually strive to make the center more desirable than the competition. Therefore, for both parties to work together, the fundamental partnership between the center and the retailer is best expressed in reasonable base rents coupled with the element of sharing that percentage rents make possible. (Percentage or overage rents are additional rents paid to the owner based on a percentage of the tenant's sales above a prearranged figure.) Such rents are an incentive to the owner-manager to bring in as many customers as possible, to run the center efficiently, and to undertake necessary new investments enthusiastically.

TENANT ROTATION

A center must change with the times — or ahead of them — to appear new, different, and fresh to its customers, especially in the face of competition. Just as merchandise changes from year to year and season to season, and department stores redesign their interior presentations, tenant shops must be refreshed and sometimes be replaced. The best way to achieve this freshness is through periodic rotation of tenants consistent with a solid plan for an attractive tenant mix. A center may be a collection of stores, but it shouldn't be a group of odds and ends.

While difficult to do in some countries and almost impossible in others, the ability to dismiss underperforming tenants, change tenant locations, and bring in new retailers is a key to the long-term success of centers everywhere. A new center or a new competitive retail format that comes into the market without a response from an existing center will do permanent and possibly fatal damage to all the tenants in the original center. Freedom to rotate tenants is fundamental to that response.

CHANGING THE LAW

When laws or regulations impede the smooth functioning of a center (when, for example, hours of operation are artificially limited or certain types of leases are not permitted), concerted efforts can be made to change the law or regulation. These efforts serve to unite all the players in a business sector who may otherwise have difficulty sharing a common cause because they are natural competitors.

COMPLETED BUILDINGS

Frequently potential center developers in countries without many existing shopping centers express an interest in buying the plans for existing centers built in other countries. But, if a Chicago shopping center were replicated in Beijing, to save the time and expense of producing new drawings, the results would very likely be financial disaster. Yet by using the common language of center development, which adds a cultural inflection, products can be truly successful.

A PORTFOLIO OF SHOPPING CENTER PROJECTS

In the foregoing pages we have discussed the common language of shopping centers and the detailed elements (the handrails, skylights, entrances, artwork) and the building blocks (the food courts, cinemas, children's play areas) that can be assembled with regional and cultural nuances to create shopping environments that are uniquely tailored to the communities they will serve. Many of the examples previously cited were taken from the following projects. These projects are all highly successful because they interpret this language in a manner befitting the center's location.

A

B

C

D

E

F

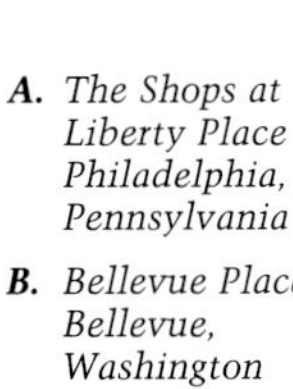

A. The Shops at Liberty Place Philadelphia, Pennsylvania

B. Bellevue Place Bellevue, Washington

C. The Gallery at Harborplace Baltimore, Maryland

D. The Shops at Liberty Place Philadelphia, Pennsylvania

E. Darling Harbourside Sydney, Australia

F. Punta Carretas Shopping Center Guipuzcoa, Montevideo, Uruguay

ANCHORAGE FIFTH AVENUE MALL
Anchorage, Alaska

A sophisticated urban retail complex located in a dark and chilly corner of North America, this center provides a sense of permanence to the largest city on America's last great frontier.

Developer: The Rainer Fund

Architect: Kober/Sclater Architects (now Sclater Kimball Architects) Seattle, Washington

Specifications: Five levels, 365,000 square feet GLA, 1,200 parking spaces

Anchors: JC Penney, Nordstrom

ARDEN FAIR
Sacramento, California

Where an existing dark and tired single-level shopping center existed, a second-level addition and horizontal expansion have increased revenue for this center fourfold. Built in the state's capitol, this project achieves institutional quality and durability with classical architectural forms.

Developer: Homart Development Co.

Architect: Altoon + Porter Architects
Los Angeles, California

Specifications: Two levels, 1,200,000 square feet GLA, 6,000 parking spaces

Anchors: Sears, Nordstrom, Weinstock's

BELLEVUE PLACE

Bellevue, Washington

This mixed-use project brought a sense of urban focus to a satellite downtown community which was struggling for identity against a much larger adjacent city. Its institutional quality has contributed to reinforcing the city's self image.

Developer: Kemper Development Company

Architect: Kober/Sclater Architects (now Sclater Kimball Architects) Seattle, Washington

Specifications: Two levels, 1,200,000 square feet GLA, 1,700 parking spaces

Anchors: The Hyatt Hotel

THE GALLERY AT HARBORPLACE

Baltimore, Maryland

Baltimore's inner harbor was a successful reclaiming of the waterside for a series of public and institutional uses. Juxtaposed to these, the Gallery creates its own sophisticated sense of destination among an already strong group of destinations.

Developer: The Rouse Company

Architect: Zeidler Roberts Partnership, Inc./Architects
Toronto, Ontario, Canada

Specifications: Four levels, 135,000 square feet GLA, 1,150 parking spaces

KAAHUMANU CENTER

Kahului, Maui, Hawaii

On a resort island known for its sumptuous tourist resort hotels, this second-level addition and expansion brought vitality to a lazy open-air mall by creating a striking new identity with unique, yet traditionally sympathetic, forms. This project has become a destination for both locals and tourists.

Developer: Maui Land & Pineapple Company, Inc.

Architect: Altoon + Porter Architects
Los Angeles, California

Specifications: Two levels, 600,000 square feet GLA, 1,400 parking spaces

Anchors: Sears, JC Penney, Liberty House

Photo courtesy David Franzen © 1995.

Photos courtesy David Franzen © 1995.

THE MALL AT GREEN HILLS

Nashville, Tennessee

Green Hills began as a strip shopping center that over several generations evolved into a complex terraced property with a confusing layout and no clear focus. This vertical and horizontal expansion brought organizational clarity to the property and repositioned a tired center into an electrifying one. At the same time traditional, local architectural style and values were maintained.

Developer: General Growth Companies, Inc.

Architect: Altoon + Porter Architects
Los Angeles, California

Specifications: Two levels, 634,316 square feet GLA, 1,177 parking spaces

Anchors: Castner-Knott, Dillard's, Gus Mayer

THE NATICK MALL
Natick, Massachusetts

Occasionally an existing single-level mall is configured in a manner that is not conducive to proper expansion. This project, a two-level superregional mall, replaces an out-of-date facility with a well-lit, dynamic, and highly competitive product.

Developer: Homart Development Co.

Architect: Arrowstreet, Inc.
Somerville, Massachusetts

Specifications: Two levels, 435,000 square feet GLA, 5,000 parking spaces

Anchors: Jordan Marsh, Filene's, Sears, Lord & Taylor

NORTH POINT MALL

Alpharetta, Georgia

In a time when few new superregional centers are being built, this project lends an air of urban civility to the suburban prototype. By creating a highly sophisticated entrance, and inventive, well-detailed interiors, North Point Mall establishes a sense of destination.

Developer: Homart Development Co.

Architect: ELS/Elbasani & Logan Architects
Berkeley, California

Specifications: Two levels, 397,000 square feet GLA, 900 parking spaces

Anchors: Sears, JC Penney, Lord & Taylor, Mervyn's, Rich's

PHIPPS PLAZA
Atlanta, Georgia

This expensive and elegant renovation/expansion has produced one of the most noteworthy image transformations in shopping center history. Up against stiff competition from an adjacent center, this new and powerful center, with elegant detailing, has caused its competition to seriously reconsider itself.

Developer: Compass Retail, Inc.
Equitable Real Estate Investment Management, Inc.

Architect: Thompson, Ventulett, Stainback & Associates, Inc.
Atlanta, Georgia

Specifications: Three levels, 825,000 square feet GLA, 4,100 parking spaces

Anchors: Parisian's, Lord & Taylor, Saks Fifth Avenue

P3

THE PLAZA AT KING OF PRUSSIA

King of Prussia, Pennsylvania

Three department stores and a major expansion and refurbishment enhanced this existing regional center. This project was transformed by incorporating elements of Philadelphia's traditional architecture, subtly blended with rich colors and materials. The result is an elegant, pleasant shopping environment.

Developer: Kravco Company

Architect: Thompson, Ventulett, Stainback & Associates, Inc.
Atlanta, Georgia

Specifications: Two levels, 1,400,000 square feet GLA, 6,711 parking spaces

Anchors: Sears, JC Penney, Nordstrom, Lord & Taylor, Neiman Marcus, Macy's, Bloomingdale's, Strawbridge & Clothier, John Wanamaker

RESTON TOWN CENTER
Reston, Virginia

Reston had developed in its first generation as a residential new town without a real heart. This town center project fulfilled the new town promise by creating a main street, a new downtown.

Developer: Reston Town Center Associates

Architect: RTKL Associates, Inc.
Baltimore, Maryland

Specifications: 220,000 square feet GLA, 1,000 parking spaces

SAINT LOUIS GALLERIA

St. Louis, Missouri

This project is a three-story expansion atrium featuring elegant restaurants, a food court, and a cinema complex on a lower level. Active fountains, hanging topiary landscape, and large umbrella columns bring special identity to this revitalized complex.

Developer: Hycel Properties Company

Architect: Hellmuth, Obata & Kassabaum, Inc.
St. Louis, Missouri

Specifications: Two levels, 1,200,000 square feet GLA, 4,814 parking spaces

Anchors: Dillard's, Famous-Barr, Lord & Taylor

THE SHOPS AT LIBERTY PLACE

Philadelphia, Pennsylvania

This urban mixed-use center combines office and retail functions that are sophisticated and a positive addition to a traditional city. Philadelphia's urban values require that the streets be walkable and that the city be perceived as cohesive. The interior spaces of this project reflect the city's proud traditions.

Developer: Rouse and Associates

Architect: Zeidler Roberts Partnership, Inc./Architects
Toronto, Ontario, Canada

Specifications: Two levels, 143,300 square feet GLA, 700 parking spaces

TOWER PLACE
Cincinnati, Ohio

Located on the city's historic shopping street, adjacent to a multi-story hotel and office complex, this three-story urban atrium is a responsible neighbor, which reinforces the look of its historic district by taking cues from projects in tighter European urban sites.

Developer: Faison Associates
Noro Realty Advisors

Architect: Altoon + Porter Architects
Los Angeles, California

Specifications: Three levels, 76,500 square feet GLA, 500 parking spaces

Anchors: The Limited, Banana Republic, The Nature Company, The Gap, Ann Taylor

MORTON'S

TRIANGLE SQUARE

Costa Mesa, California

Located on a triangular-shaped site, bounded by three highly trafficked streets, this urban redevelopment project needed to create three fronts and three corners with no backside. What resulted is a collection of destinations including entertainment, dining, focused retailing, and relaxation.

Developer: Triangle Square Joint Venture

Architect: Altoon + Porter Architects
Los Angeles, California

Specifications: Two levels, 200,000 square feet GLA, 1,064 parking spaces

Anchors: The Gap, Nike Town, Virgin Megastore,
Edwards 8-Plex Cinemas, Barnes & Noble Booksellers,
Alpha Beta Supermarket, restaurants

TRIANGLE SQUARE
GAP
GAP

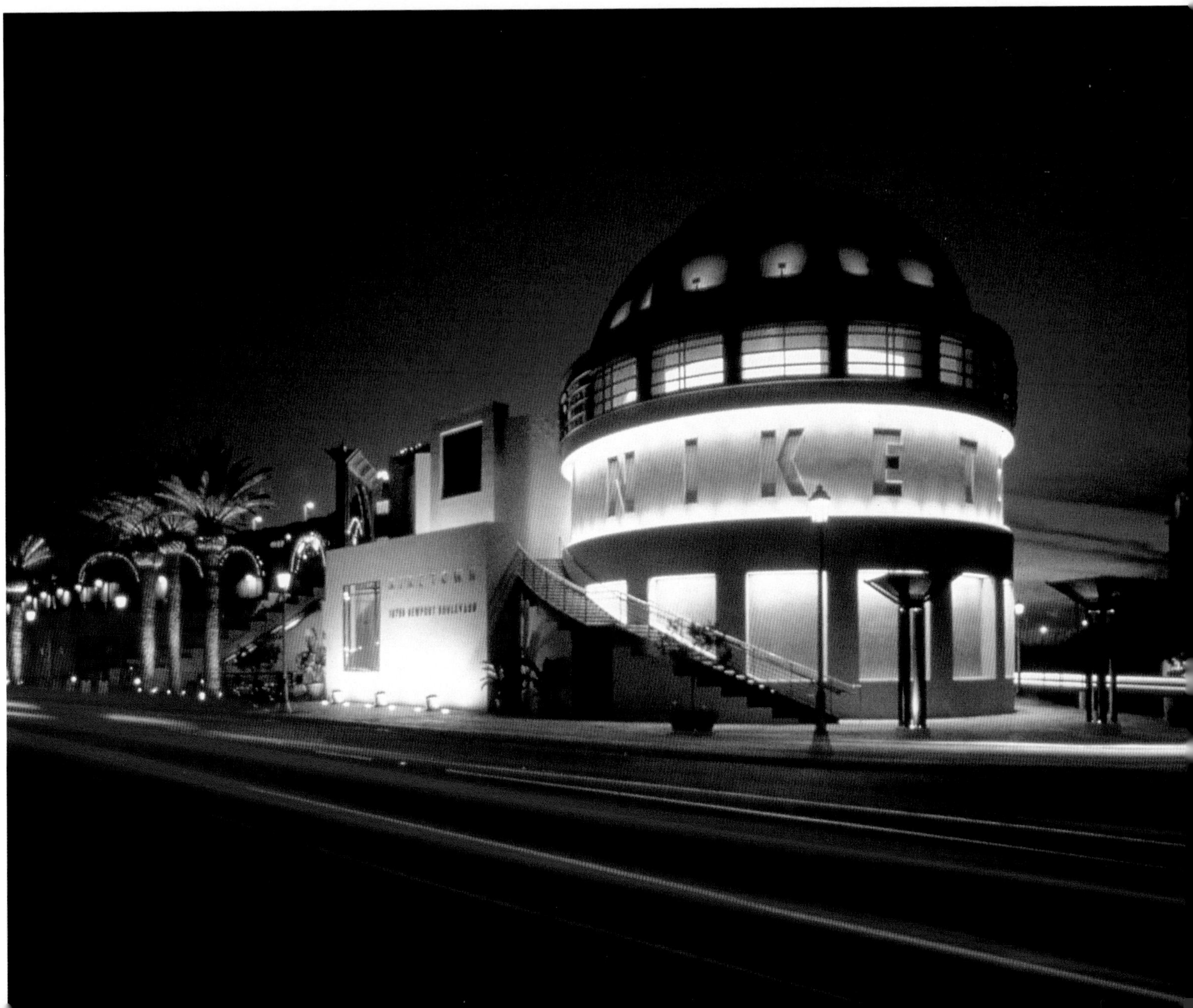

UNIVERSAL CITYWALK

Universal City, California

Located among a collection of superregional magnets, including a world class studio and backlot tour, an amusement park, an enclosed amphitheater, two large hotels, the region's largest cinema, and a restaurant row, this project places entertainment before retail, yet creates a unique destination in a community known for its eccentricities. With merchandise found more frequently in tourist traps and less often in fashion centers, CityWalk has become a solid social outlet for locals, while attracting tourists from around the world.

Developer: MCA Development Company

Architect: The Jerde Partnership, Inc.
Santa Monica, California

Specifications: One level, 200,000 square feet GLA, 2,400 parking spaces

Anchors: The Nature Company, Universal City Cinemas-Cineplex Odeon, Universal Studios Hollywood Theme Park, Sam Goody

KWGB
JUICE

VALENCIA TOWN CENTER
Valencia, California

Providing both interior and exterior public space amenities, this center completed the promise of a new town, which began as a bedroom community. With strong architectural form, gracious open space amenities, Town Center interacts well with the adjacent community.

Developer:	The Newhall Land and Farming Company JMB Retail Properties Company
Architect:	RTKL Associates Inc. Los Angeles, California
Specifications:	Two levels, 281,209 square feet GLA, 3,700 parking spaces
Anchors:	JC Penney, Sears, Robinson's/May Company

VALENCIA
TOWN CENTER
DIRECTORY
Thanksgiving

WORCESTER COMMON FASHION OUTLETS

Worcester, Massachusetts

This is a successful conversion of an urban regional mall into an enclosed two-level outlet center. In addition to strong anchors, this project has an inventive and colorful environmental graphic design and signage program that creates a special ambiance.

Developer: New England Development

Architect: Arrowstreet, Inc.
Somerville, Massachusetts

Specifications: Two levels, 348,610 square feet GLA, 4,000 parking spaces

Anchors: Saks Clearinghouse, Filene's Basement, Sports Authority, Media Play, Bed, Bath & Beyond

au bon pain
FRIENDLY

ERIN MILLS TOWN CENTRE

Mississauga, Ontario

This regional center is organized around a radial layout featuring a 150-foot high clock tower with clarion, a nine-hole interior putting green, and a four-sided, 256-screen video display. With polychromatic coloring inside and out, this project is both serious and playful as a shopping environment.

Developer: Cadillac Fairview Corporation, Ltd.

Architect: RTKL Associates Inc.
Baltimore, Maryland

Specifications: Two levels, 663,000 square feet GLA, 4,060 parking spaces

Anchors: Eaton's, Sears, Hudson Bay

CIBC Banking Centre
CIBC

HAMILTON EATON CENTRE
Hamilton, Ontario

Hamilton Eaton Centre is a three-level galleria whose exterior recreates the traditional architecture of Eaton's former store. Linked by bridges to adjacent blocks, this project provides an all-weather environment in a place where winter strikes with severity.

Developer: Cadillac Fairview Corporation and Eaton Properties

Architect: RTKL International, Ltd.
Baltimore, Maryland

Specifications: Three levels, 411,000 square feet GLA, 825 parking spaces

Anchors: Eaton's

EATON CENTRE

SHERWAY GARDENS
Etobicoke, Ontario

Against the backdrop of a circus-like tent ceiling, this sophisticated and skillfully executed design repositions the center, leaving no doubt about the quality of the building and the product.

Developer: The Rouse Company
Canada Life Assurance Company, Ltd.

Architect: Zeidler Roberts Partnership, Inc./Architects
Toronto, Ontario, Canada

Specifications: Two levels, 132,000 square feet GLA, 5,700 parking spaces

Anchors: Brettons

PLAZA DEL ATLANTICO

Arecibo

Utilizing the floor as a painter's canvas, with some bold ceiling forms accented by neon, this renovation repositions an older single-level regional mall into a more stimulating and exciting shopping environment.

Developer: Manley-Berenson Associates, Inc.

Architect: Arrowstreet, Inc.
Somerville, Massachusetts

Specifications: One level, 190,000 square feet GLA, 1,000 parking spaces

Anchors: Capri, Kmart

ALE
%
off
ALE

PLAZA RIO HONDO
Bayamón

In a culture that enjoys a colorful environmental palette, and against the backdrop of playful architectural forms, this project with a very modest budget renovates and repositions a single-level regional mall in a manner that is enticing and adventuresome.

Developer: Manley-Berenson Associates, Inc.

Architect: Arrowstreet, Inc.
Somerville, Massachusetts

Specifications: One level, 295,000 square feet GLA, 2,000 parking spaces

Anchors: Woolworth, La Giralda

GiRALDA

CENTRO COMERCIAL SANTA FE

Mexico City

Built on an 88-acre site, which was previously a stone quarry, this three-level terraced mall attempts to implant an American prototype into the Mexican shopping culture. In an effort to be sensitive to Mexico's tradition of heavy stone buildings, heavy and obtrusive stone bridges challenge customers by obstructing the sight lines.

Developer: Desc. Societead de Formento Industrial

Architect: Hellmuth, Obata & Kassabaum, Inc.
St. Louis, Missouri

Specifications: Three levels, 1,070,000 square feet GLA, 6,800 parking spaces

Anchors: Palacio de Hiero, Liverpool

ESTACION TERMINAL DE OMNIBUS Y CENTRO COMERCIAL TUCUMAN

San Miguel de Tucumán

This project integrates an urban regional transit node with a shopping center designed as an open air project. When completed, it will house a supermarket, an amusement park, regional shops, food court, and 160 in-line retail units.

Developer: Terminal del Tucumán S.A.

Architect: Juan Carlos Lopez & Asociados S.A.
Buenos Aires, Argentina

Specifications: One level, 344,448 square feet GLA, 750 parking spaces

Anchors: Disco Supermarket

PARQUE ARAUCO
Santiago de Chile

A refurbishment to an existing center converted a narrow, dark space into a much more inviting one, through the introduction of a glazed skylight vault, elaborate lighting, new ceilings, vertical circulation, and a major new entrance.

Developer: Parque Arauco S.A.

Architect: Juan Carlos Lopez & Asociados S.A.
Buenos Aires, Argentina

Specifications: Three levels, 861,120 square feet GLA, 3,500 parking spaces

Anchors: Almacenes Paris, Ripley, Falabella

SISLEY
SISLEY
ALMACENES PARIS

PUNTA CARRETAS SHOPPING CENTER

Guipuzcoa, Montevideo

This unique and unusual design opportunity allowed the owners to refurbish the old city jail, converting it into a shopping center, convention center, and international hotel. Not only do the remnant architectural elements enrich the quality of space, but the curiosity of converting a jail into a free market mecca is most enticing.

Developer: Alian S.A.

Architect: Juan Carlos Lopez & Asociados S.A.
Buenos Aires, Argentina

Specifications: Three levels, 753,480 square feet GLA, 1,100 parking spaces

Anchors: Disco Supermarket, Opera

RINGSTRASSEN GALERIEN

Vienna

Built at two stages by separate architect/development teams, this project creates a strong and sophisticated urban galleria located along Vienna's famed Ringstrasse. The rich materials, rich food, and the scale of the project provide a venue for a quiet interlude as a respite from a very formal city.

Developer:	Part 1: Winterthur Versicherungs AG Part 2: Corso Bauprojekt Management GmbH
Architect:	Part 1: Wilhelm Holzbauer + Georg Lippert Part 2: Neumann + Hlaveniczka + Lintl + Partner
Specifications:	Three levels, 36,090 square feet, 750 parking spaces
Anchors:	Mövenpick, BML - Group (Billa)

THE BENTALL CENTRE
Kingston Upon Thames

Bentalls Department Store was redeveloped to create The Bentall Centre, comprised of the new six-story Bentalls Department Store and a shopping center on four floors beneath a glazed galleria. Rich interior finishes confirm the institutional message of the grand entry to the street.

Developer: The Norwich Union Life Insurance Society in partnership with Bentalls plc

Architect: Building Design Partnership

Specifications: Three levels, 183,727 square feet, 1,200 parking spaces

Anchors: Bentalls Department Store, WH Smith, Dillons, HMV

Bentalls
Bentalls

HEUVEL GALERIE
Eindhoven

This traditional glazed galleria shopping center is noteworthy for its contrast between playful, sophisticated graphics and its formal and heavy architecture. The glass galleria overhead brings welcome relief to the heavy masonry structure below.

Developer: MAB B.V.

Architect: Walter Brune architectur/Aken B.V. Architectur & Stedebouw

Specifications: Three levels, 85,300 square feet, 1,160 parking spaces

Anchors: Hennes & Mauritz Intertoys, Van Piere Boeken, De Jong Supermarkt

Slot

CLARKE QUAY
Singapore

In a city known for its contemporary economic and building achievements, this sensitive commitment to reinvest in the city's historic waterfront has resulted in a delightful district of living history. This enticing project, while largely focused on restaurants, is a welcome addition to the neighborhood.

Developer: Clarke Quay Pte Ltd

Architects: ELS/Elbasani & Logan Architects
Berkeley, California

RSP Architects, Planners & Engineers
Singapore

Specifications: Three levels, 189,873 square feet GLA, 400 parking spaces

Anchors: Clarke Quay Adventure, Sogo Department Store, Wang Jiang Lou Yunnan Kitchen

HIMEJI RIVERCITY CENTER
Himeji

Located in a largely blue collar city with an emerging middle class, this project tries to capitalize on an increasing amount of leisure time and pent up demand for consumer goods. This three-level mall is simple in concept and provides substantially less merchandising energy than most projects designed today. Noticeably absent are environmental graphics, inventive signage and storefronts, decorative lighting, artwork, and many of the mechanisms employed to bring scale to a shopping center.

Developer: Jusco Company, Ltd.

Architect: Hellmuth, Obata & Kassabaum, Inc.
St. Louis, Missouri

Specifications: Three levels, 750,000 square feet GLA

Anchors: Jusco Department Store

CITRALAND MALL
Jakarta

Conceived as a multi-use center that contains a large hotel, this eight-level spiral-ramp shopping atrium, is situated on a site large enough to allow it to exist on three levels. Its dramatic atrium space is challenged by a level of detail that would not satisfy fashion retailers in North America.

Developer: Ciputra Group

Architect: D. I. Architecture Inc.
Baltimore, Maryland

Specifications: Eight Levels, 630,340 square feet GLA, 3,500 parking spaces

Anchors: Department store, Citraland Hotel

CITRALAND
HOTEL
CITRALAND

PONDOK INDAH MALL
Jakarta

American in layout, this three-level mall is anchored by department stores, supermarkets, and a food court. With customary surface parking in the front, this project establishes nighttime identity through prolific use of tenant signage and neon.

Developer: P.T. Metropolitan Kencana

Architect: Development Design Group, Inc.
Baltimore, Maryland

Specifications: Three levels, 400,090 square feet GLA, 2,200 parking spaces

Anchors: Metro Department Store, Cinema 21,
Jakarta Electronics Center, Office Metro, Toys City

CHADSTONE CENTRE
Chadstone, Victoria

With a striking two-tiered center-court dome, this two-level addition with a two-level and one-level galleria is a formal, exciting, and classical destination.

Developer: The Gandel Group of Companies

Architect: RTKL International, Ltd.
Baltimore, Maryland

Specifications: Two levels, 48,100 square meters GLA, 4,000 parking spaces

Anchors: Myer, Target, Coles New World, McEdwans

FISH & GRILL

DARLING HARBOURSIDE

Sydney

Strongly reminiscent of Harbor Place in Baltimore, this project brings the elements of a festival market, with interior and exterior dining, to a renovated waterfront. Rich with art elements and harbor related activities, this project is linked to a rapid transit system and to a new hotel across the street.

Developer: Merlin International Properties Ltd.
The Enterprise Development Company

Architect: RTKL International, Ltd.
Baltimore, Maryland

Specifications: Two levels, 150,000 square feet GLA

THE GALLERIA MORLEY
Perth

A 30-meter wide octagonal central atrium is the focus of this major regional shopping center. Classical and formal, its central fountain creates a destination within a destination.

Developer: Coles Myer Properties, Ltd.

Architect: RTKL Associates Inc.
Los Angeles, California

Specifications: Three levels, 39,800 square meters GLA, 3,500 parking spaces

Anchors: Kmart, Target, Myer

SPORTSGIRL CENTRE
Melbourne

Situated on an avenue on a tight urban site, this eleven-story atrium contains retail at the lower levels. A sophisticated design is reinforced by dramatic lighting, and the center makes a solid contribution to the urban fabric.

Developer:	Sportscraft Proprietary, Ltd.
Architect:	Anthony Belluschi Architects, Inc. Chicago, Illinois
Specifications:	Four levels, 5,600 square meters GLA
Anchors:	Sportsgirl

AL HARTHY COMPLEX

Muscat

Part of a multi-use project, this 13,000 square meter retail center attempts to formalize retailing in a part of the world where trading has always been synonymous with life. A prominent exterior main entry is more emblematic of a government building, but the interior has been designed to encourage family shopping.

Developer:	Al Ghurair Group
Architect:	Auscon Engineering & Architecture Sultanate of Oman
Specifications:	Three levels, 13,000 square meters GLA
Anchors:	OuiSet/Oui

BUR JUMAN CENTRE
Dubai

Utilizing decorative lighting, scenic elevators, illuminated glass block floors, and an active graphics program, this project caters to the upper-middle and upper segments of the population. Featuring stores such as Christian Dior, Escada, Bally, Benneton, Esprit, Liz Claiborne, Warner, Hallmark, and JC Penney, it provides a range of merchandise for both locals and expatriates.

Developer: Al Ghurair Group

Architect: D. I. Architecture, Inc.
Baltimore, Maryland

Specifications: Five levels, 1,000,000 square feet GLA, 1,500 parking spaces

Anchors: JC Penney, BHS, Fashion Way, Next, Lal's Supermarket

AL GHURAIR CENTRE

Dubai

First built in 1979 as part of a multi-purpose complex with apartments and office buildings, the shopping center now includes 300 retail shops. At this scale, this project serves as a crossroads market for many people in the Southern Hemisphere.

Developer: Al Ghurair Group

Architect: D. I. Architecture, Inc.
United Kingdom

Specifications: Ten levels, 320,000 square feet GLA, 1,300 parking spaces

Anchors: McDonald's, four stores, and supermarkets

CONCLUSION

From an examination of shopping centers around the globe, it is clear that the difference between success and failure is directly related to the understanding of the elements that form the basic structure of these projects and the details from which they are crafted. Without a doubt, there are more failures than successes. There is a greater instinct to build inexpensively than to build correctly.

But what is also clear is that developers from different cultures can learn about common issues and details from one another. By understanding the common language of shopping centers and multi-use projects and by appreciating that these projects must be rooted deeply within the cultures that these buildings will serve, developers can create projects that will be successful for many generations to come.

This book has been intended as a primer and as a mechanism to facilitate clear understanding of the elements upon which successful retailing centers are built. What may look successful in one environment may only be an illusion. The importance of bringing all the elements together — the business deal, the merchants, architectural design, the programs, relationship to the community — cannot be underestimated. Successful projects can be achieved by understanding and speaking a common shopping center language.

A

B

C

D

E

F

A. *Floating Market Bangkok, Thailand*

B. *Darling Harbourside Sydney, Australia*

C. *Kaahumanu Center Kahului, Maui, Hawaii Photo courtesy David Franzen © 1995.*

D. *Arden Fair Sacramento, California*

E. *Lincolnwood Town Center Lincolnwood, Illinois*

F. *Basket Market Guadalajara, Mexico*